CRYPTID CREATURES

LEARN TO DRAW MYSTERIOUS BEASTS
FROM AROUND THE WORLD

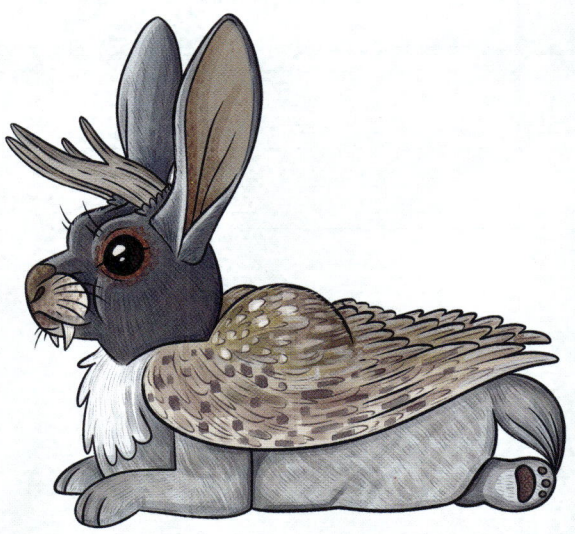

Ballyraven

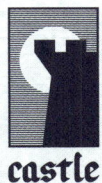

castle

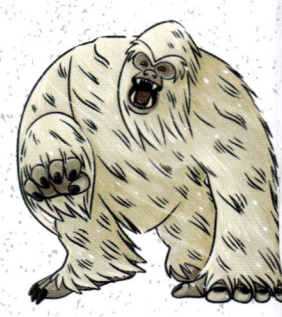

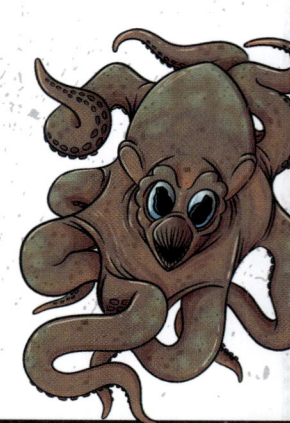

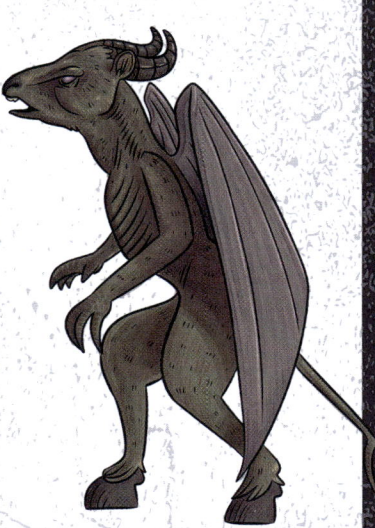

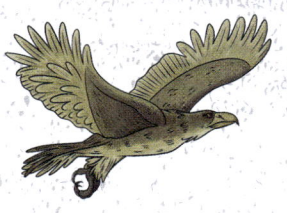

Come with Me on a Cryptid Drawing Journey

Hello!

My name is Kristen, but most people online know me by my alter-ego, Ballyraven (a blue, cryptid-hunting, magical bird). I've been drawing monsters and fantastical things for as long as I can remember—and have always been enthralled by cryptids. After receiving a BFA from the University of Alaska Fairbanks, I worked as a freelance illustrator, painter, and ceramicist. I set up my artist's booth at the Mothman Festival for the first time in 2017 to exhibit and sell artwork; I have since become known for my cryptid anatomy sketches.

Today, my work revolves solely around folklore, cryptids, and mythical creatures. Through Patreon, I run a fictitious organization called the Ballyraven Cryptid Wildlife Protection Agency (BCWPA), where I publish illustrations, comics, literature, videos, and all the research that goes into them. Through the BCWPA, I hope to share my love for not only cryptids but also nature and making things.

For this book, I have put together only a small sample of the most popular cryptids from around the world. Hopefully you will see a few of your favorites, and a few you've never heard of. Once you've read and drawn all thirty-five, your cryptid adventure doesn't have to end; there are many more cryptids to discover everywhere (and likely at least one local to you)!

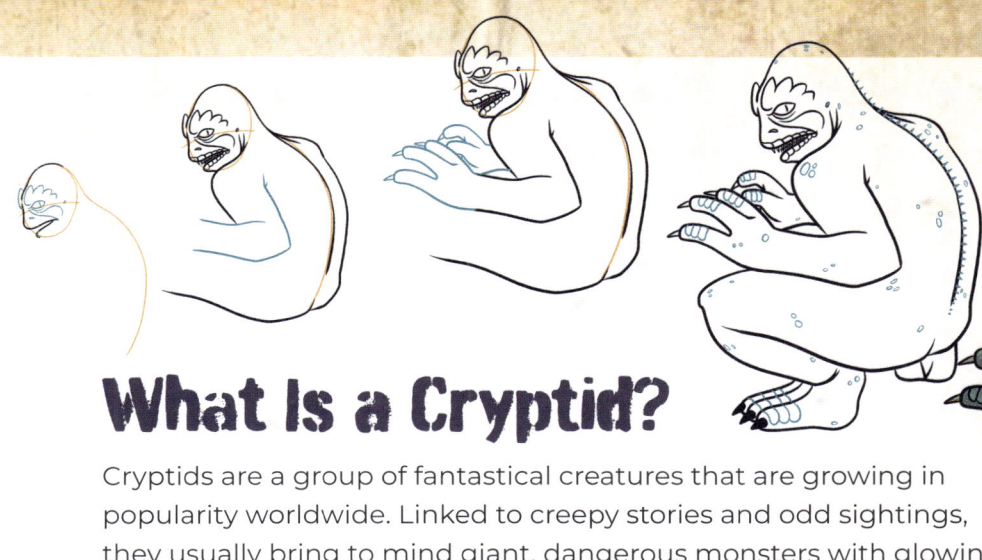

What Is a Cryptid?

Cryptids are a group of fantastical creatures that are growing in popularity worldwide. Linked to creepy stories and odd sightings, they usually bring to mind giant, dangerous monsters with glowing eyes. What exactly a cryptid is, though, is controversial. There is no agreement on what can or cannot be a cryptid, so everyone has a different opinion.

Some people regard cryptids as real animals that have evaded scientific study and capture; those who believe in and search for these organisms are called cryptozoologists. The most well-known cryptozoology teams hunt for Sasquatch (also known as Bigfoot), the Loch Ness Monster, and the Michigan Dogman. Many of these groups also label aliens that have visited Earth as cryptids (the Flatwoods Monster, Hopkinsville Goblin, and Grinning Man).

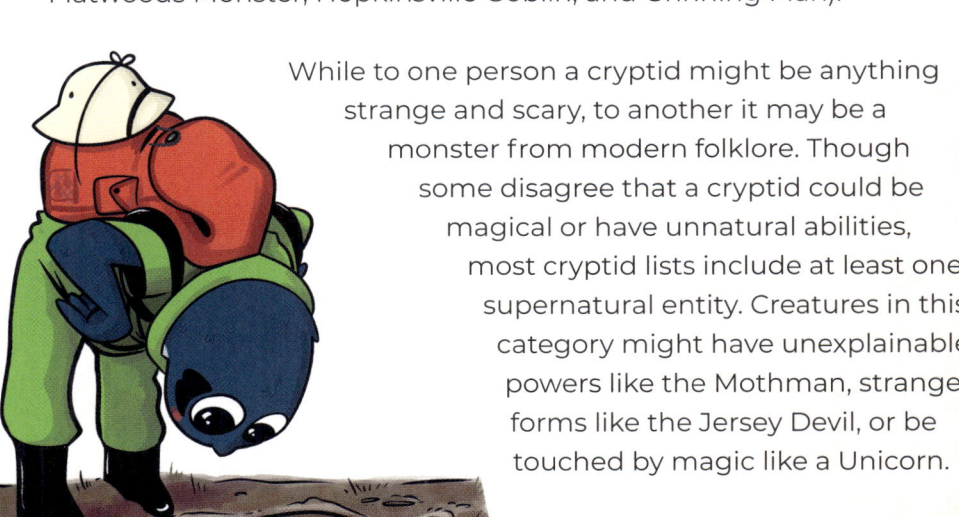

While to one person a cryptid might be anything strange and scary, to another it may be a monster from modern folklore. Though some disagree that a cryptid could be magical or have unnatural abilities, most cryptid lists include at least one supernatural entity. Creatures in this category might have unexplainable powers like the Mothman, strange forms like the Jersey Devil, or be touched by magic like a Unicorn.

Even broader definitions of cryptid exist. On some lists, one can find ancient beasts that people of the past believed in, paranormal monsters, part-human entities, and beings of nature. It isn't unusual to include fake cryptids, either. Fearsome critters and hoax animals, like the Hodag and Fiji Mermaid, are a treasured part of cryptid history despite their ties to trickery.

The definition of cryptid is as hard to pin down as the subjects they discuss. However, all can agree a cryptid is a living being that most people have not seen, and something not (or not *entirely*) human. For the entries in this book, I have compiled a list of entities most people agree to be cryptids. This list features creatures that have been observed or encountered and have a dedicated base of believers. You will also find a few cryptid hoaxes. Originating from fabricated events, these deceptions tricked people into believing in them and spawned genuine reports. Nevertheless, there are no right or wrong answers to the question, "what is a cryptid?" What does "cryptid" mean to you?

Drawing Tools

One of the best things about drawing is that you can do it in any medium you're comfortable with: pencils, crayons, markers, ink pens, or even paint. For beginning artists, it is best to start simply with a pencil and eraser. While you can use whatever you have on hand or like best, here are my go-to tools.

Traditional Drawing

For most of my work, I use any #2 mechanical pencil I can find. With light pressure, it can produce a vague sketch; with a lot of force, it can also make dark lines. However, when I am looking for something more complex, having a few different graphite grades is best.

A graphite grade is a small code found near the end of your pencil. It is made up of a letter and a number. This code will tell you if you are holding a pencil that will make a lightly colored mark or a dark line. H to H9 make increasingly fainter lines; this is because the lead is harder (hence the H). H pencils are the perfect pencil to start any drawing with because they are easy to erase and can fade into the background when paired with bolder lines. B to B9 pencils (B for "black") make increasingly darker lines. These pencils are used to make your final lines.

If you have a pencil pack, you may also have a pencil marked F or HB. Both of these pencils are mid-level shades. F pencils are lighter than HB and B but darker than H; fine-point pencils, stay sharper than the other darker pencils and are great for shading or adding texture to a drawing. HB is the shade in the middle of the graphite scale. The #2 pencils commonly used in American schools are HB pencils.

Aside from pencils, you will also need a pencil sharpener and a good eraser. If you can, purchase an eraser separate from your pencil; the red ones that usually come attached to pencils may smudge (and not erase) your marks, leave red residue behind, and can often tear the paper. My favorite eraser is a kneaded eraser; sort of like a ball of putty, it can remove both light and dark lines without damage. It can also be broken into small pieces to erase very specific or small areas, as well as be rolled over the top of your drawing to lighten a sketch.

For your final lines, you may want to use an ink pen or marker to make dark, bold lines instead of a B pencil. When I use ink, I prefer Micron pens. A pack includes a few different sized tips, so you can draw small details and thick outlines. If you plan on using wet mediums to color your drawings, make sure to use waterproof inks.

When coloring your cryptids, you can color right on top of your pencil marks. Colored pencils, crayons, and markers work great: Once you've colored in your drawing, you can go over your lines again with a dark marker or pen to make the artwork pop. Alternatively, you can use watercolor paint, diluted inks, or pastel markers to color on top of your drawing; these tools are see-through, so going over your lines again wouldn't be necessary.

While you can easily draw on almost any kind of paper, plan ahead if you want to include paints or markers. Specific papers are available that work best with these mediums. Try testing out different sketch pads; containing forty to one hundred sheets of paper, you will not only have plenty of pages to draw on, but you'll also become familiar with each type of paper and how best to use them. For pencil drawings, I recommend any wire-bound drawing pad, as they lay flat and are the easiest to draw on. However, it's good to practice with and try as many drawing tools as possible to see what you like best.

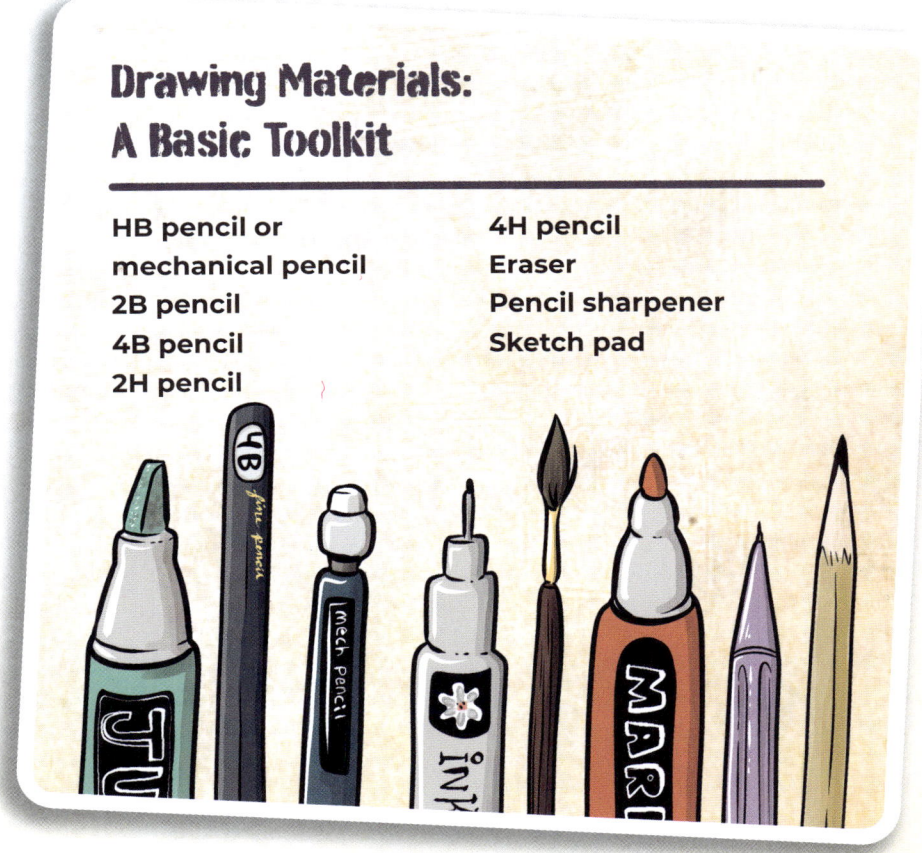

Drawing Materials: A Basic Toolkit

HB pencil or mechanical pencil
2B pencil
4B pencil
2H pencil

4H pencil
Eraser
Pencil sharpener
Sketch pad

Digital Drawing

Some people prefer to draw digitally on a computer or tablet. Many programs are available for laptops, desktops, and iPads, but my favorite combination is Clip Studio on an XPPen graphic tablet. Drawing on a graphic tablet feels more like drawing on paper than other digital methods, but if that isn't as comfortable for you, you may enjoy drawing with a mouse or your finger instead.

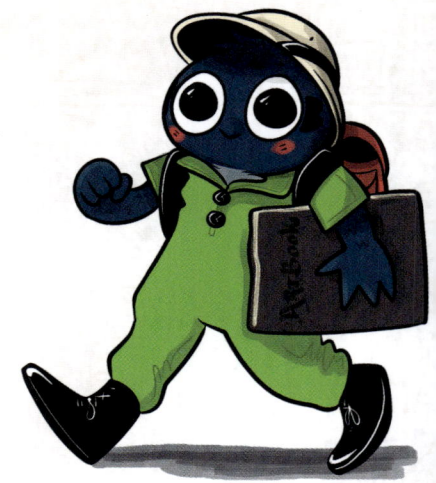

Drawing Tips

Now that you have all your tools, let's discuss how to use them! These tips and techniques will help you draw all the creatures in this book—and go beyond just drawing them. The topics covered below, including sketching, basic shapes and forms, lines, and textures will be used in the book's step-by-step guides; read over them carefully to understand how we progress from start to finish when drawing a cryptid.

Sketching

Sketching is how you begin a new drawing. To sketch, lightly draw by barely touching the paper with your pencil or applying little pressure; you can make the best sketches with H pencils. Sketches help you plan out what you'll draw where. Drawing lightly also enables you to figure out tricky shapes or angles. Sketches are erased, so don't worry about making them perfect. Use them as guides for your drawing.

In this book's step-by-step tutorials, sketch lines are colored orange.

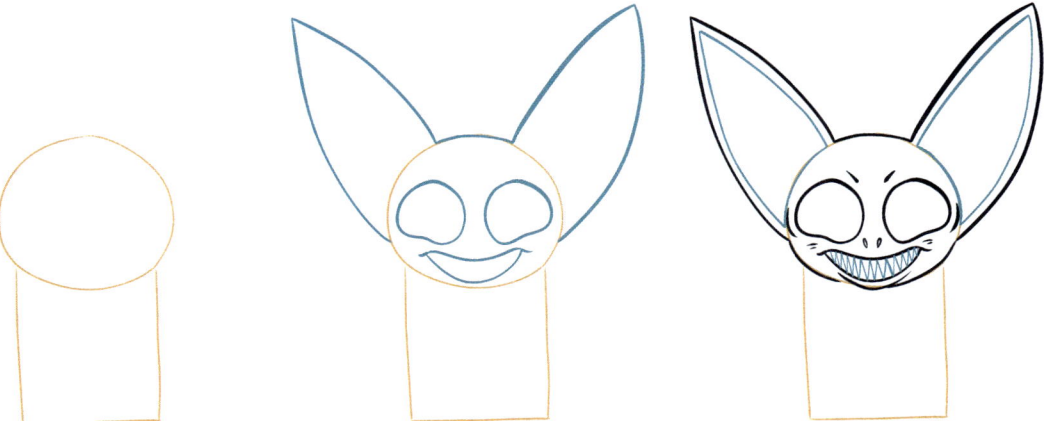

Basic Shapes and Forms

When starting a cryptid drawing, the first step is to plan it out. Everything you draw can be broken down into basic shapes: circles, triangles, and rectangles. We can sketch shapes to build a cryptid and plan where its head, limbs, and other parts go. As these basic shapes and forms are part of a sketch, they will be erased near the end of the drawing process. These shapes and lines will work as a guide to draw other, permanent lines.

Lines

We use many types of lines to make a drawing! Aside from shape, lines also vary in color and thickness. As we talked about (on pages 7-8), sketch lines are thin and will be light gray marks on your paper. When we draw anything that has a face, we also sketch guidelines. Made up of one horizontal and one vertical line, they curve around the subject's head; guidelines help artists accurately visualize and place facial features.

The second stage of drawing is made up of rough draft lines. These lines are a bit thicker and more visible than sketch lines but still easily erasable; they may expand upon or alter a sketch. Rough

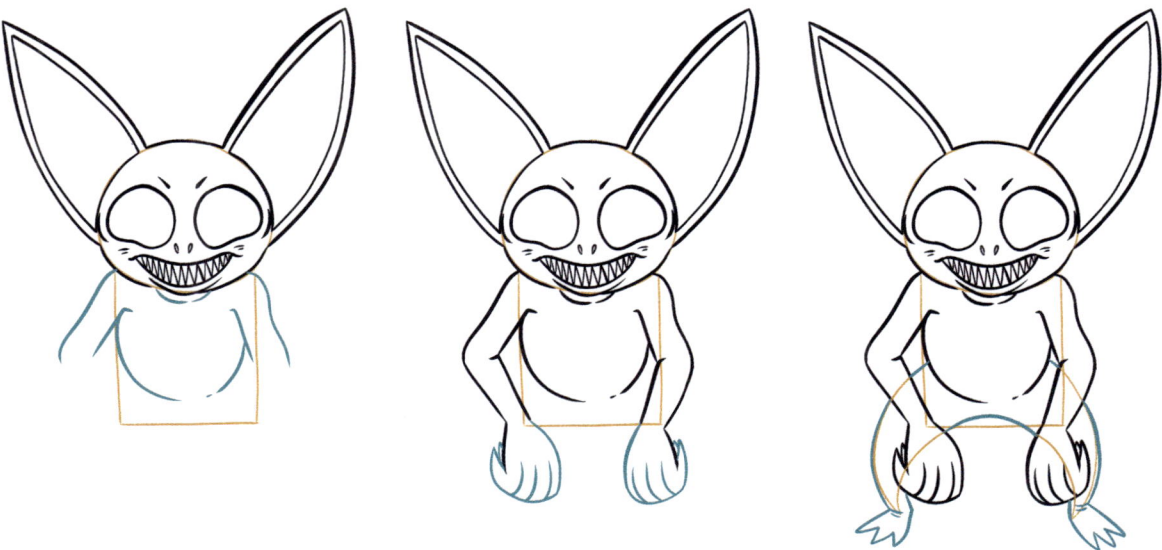

draft lines are replaced by the final set of lines: line art. Line art can be the last stage of drawing if shading or coloring won't be added, and is made up of thick, bold lines. When these final lines are drawn, all others are erased.

In the step-by-step drawings, the rough draft steps are omitted for simplicity. When following this book's tutorials, lightly draw your line art lines first, then go over them with a bold pencil or pen. Practicing this method will help you plan and draw from your imagination.

In this book's step-by-step tutorials, each step of added line art will be colored blue; previous steps of completed line art will be denoted by black lines.

Textures

Textures are series or patterns of lines; they are the last step in finishing line art. Textures are lines that hint at hair, scales, and other details, and most are made by repeating a few short, similar lines or shapes. Textures are also considered line art, so they are made up of bold lines. You can see several examples of texture under Fur and Hide of the Additional Resources.

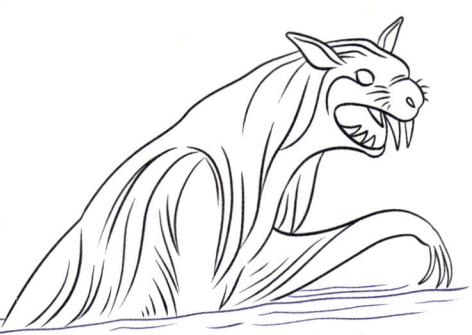
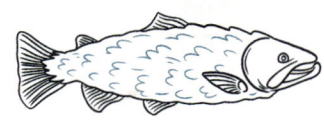
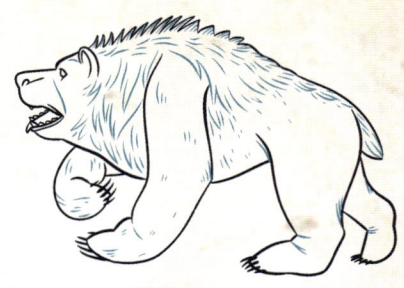
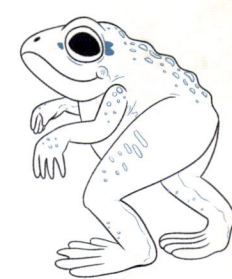

Drawing in the Field

Cryptids are usually just animals with odd characteristics, strange powers, or that are unusually big. One of the best ways to practice drawing cryptids is to practice drawing animals. While looking at reference pictures and drawing them is good practice, taking your drawing tools outside is more fun.

Try taking a sketchpad or whatever you draw with outside and looking at animals around you. Many cryptids have an animal they are similar to, like Thunderbirds (page 178) and hawks, Mothman (page 170) and moths, or Hellhounds (page 144) and dogs. Learning about animals and practicing drawing them will help you imagine what a cryptid might look like. Carry a sketchbook to practice wherever you go! Zoos and museums are great places to see rare animals.

It also helps to familiarize yourself with habitats. Walking around your neighborhood or visiting parks will help you draw backgrounds and think about how to pose or color your cryptid.

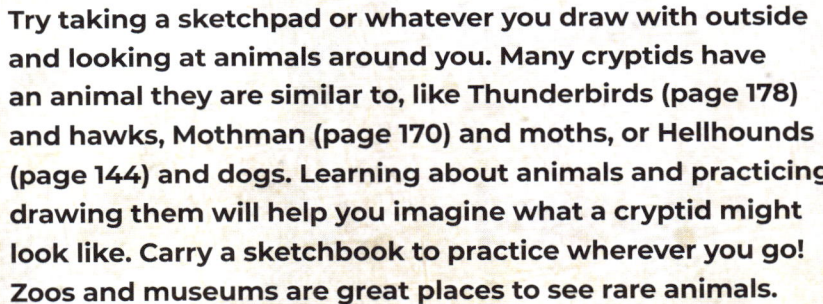
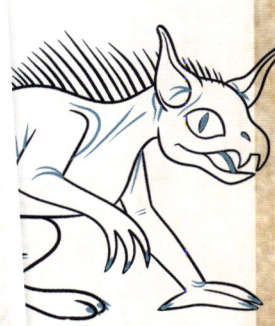
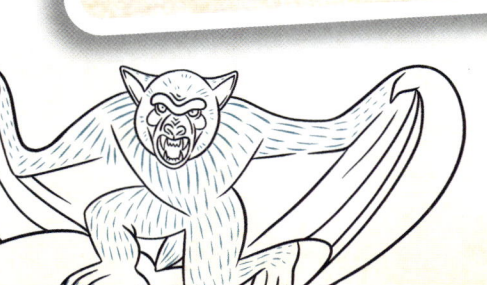
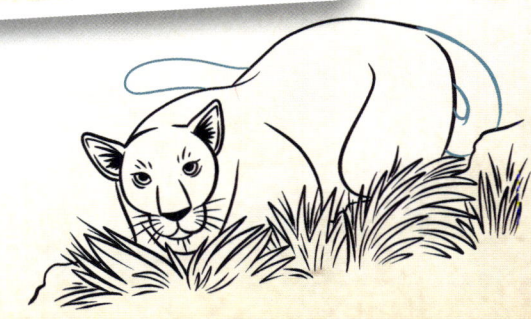

A BEGINNER'S GUIDE
TO CRYPTIDS

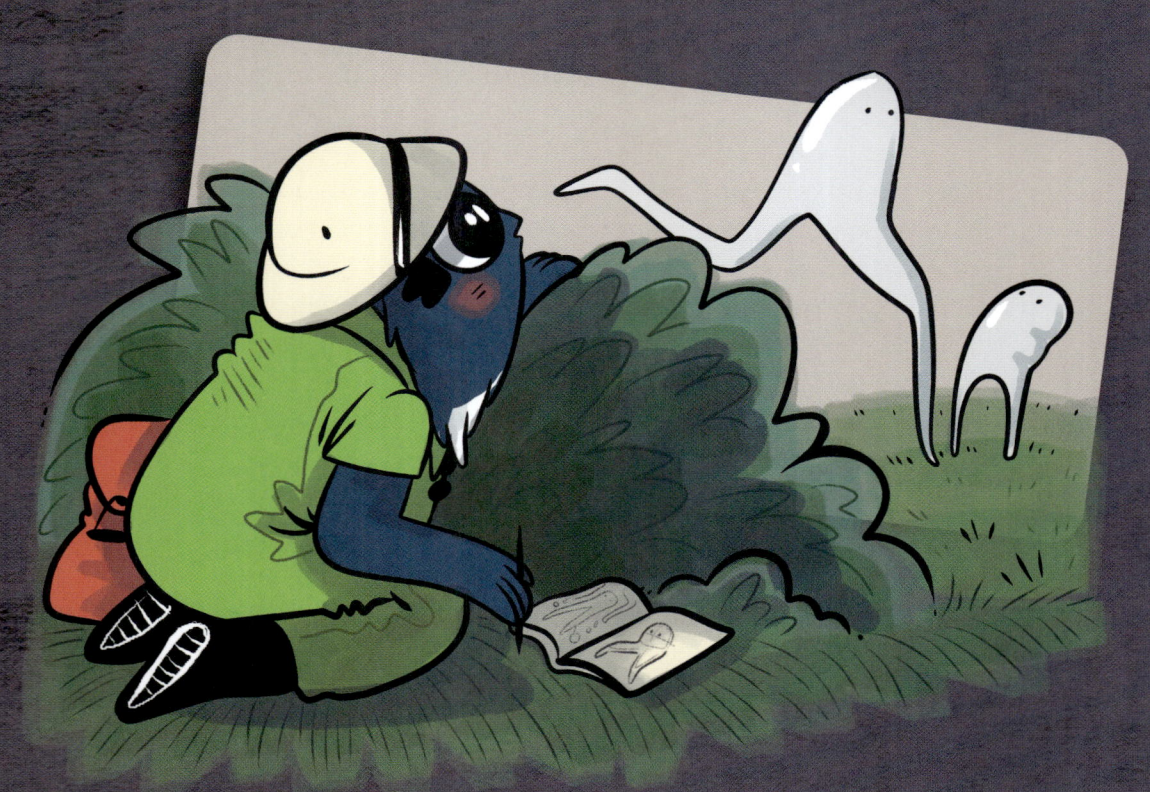

There are hundreds of cryptids from around the world; in fact, there are so many that it would be difficult to draw every one of them. In this book, I'll only teach you how to draw some of the most famous—but that doesn't mean you can't try to draw them all! While each cryptid is unique, many share a lot of similarities; most can be separated into one of five common cryptid types. Learning to draw one of each type will make drawing others like it much easier.

Common Types of Cryptids

Cryptids generally fall under one of five categories: Bigfoot, Lake Monster, Half-Human Monster, Odd Animal, or Prehistoric Animal.

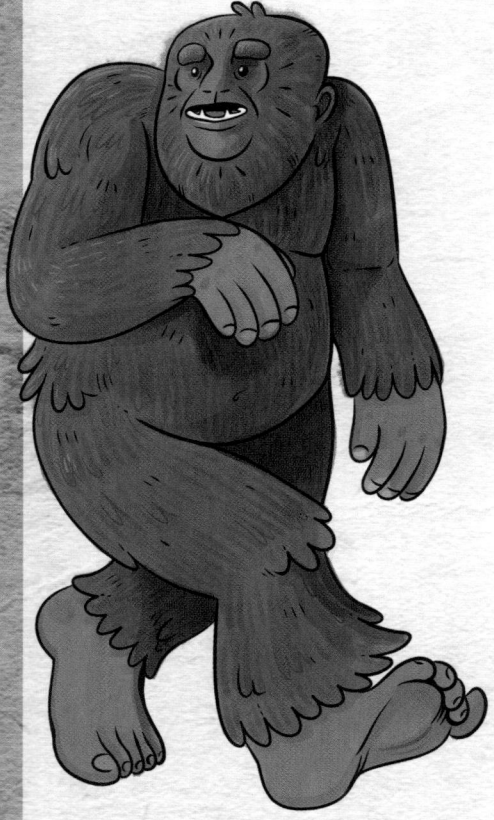

Bigfoot

Large, hairy creatures with human, ape, or monkey-like faces fall into the Bigfoot category. These cryptids usually walk on two legs and have no tail. Beings in this category are broad, strong, and often have hairless hands, faces, and feet. Many cryptids are just like Bigfoot (also known and named in this book as Sasquatch, see page 82), except they have another animal's face or are smaller in size. Bigfoot examples include the Yeti (page 54), Yahoo, Albatwitch, and Alma.

Lake Monster

Cryptids from lakes are generally described as giant snakes or plesiosaurs (which are similar to snakes with full bellies and flippers). They are known to have long necks, beady eyes, and mouths full of sharp teeth. They loop in and out of the water. Lake monster examples include the Loch Ness Monster (page 94), Bozho, Champ, and Kusshii.

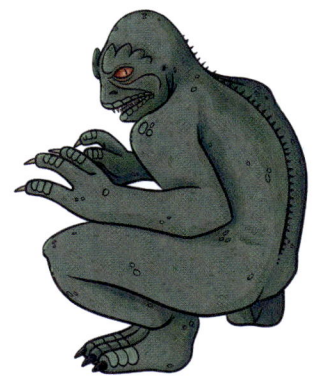

Half-Human Monster

Often featuring "-man" at the end of their name, half-human monsters have human torsos and humanlike legs or feet. These cryptids are usually described as being intelligent and a little magical; they can also generally be summarized as anthropomorphic animals. Half-human monster examples include the Kentucky Goatman (page 148), Mothman (page 170), Cornish Owlman, and Dogman.

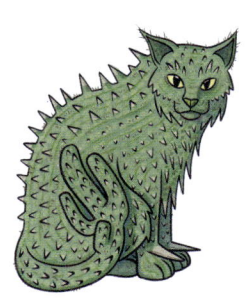

Odd Animal

Some cryptids are just like any other animal—*except* for one weird thing. This can be growing horns, wings, a second head, or reaching an enormous size—or just existing somewhere they shouldn't. Odd animal examples include the Ogua (page 112), Tuttle Creek Manatee, Snarly Yow, and Sheepsquatch.

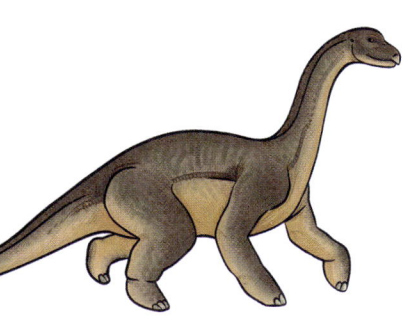

Prehistoric Animal

Dinosaurs, Ice Age animals, and other extinct creatures make up a large percentage of cryptids. While they can vary in body type and appearance, reference sources and scientific illustrations are available to help you draw those that fall into this category. Lake monsters and odd animals sometimes overlap with this category. Prehistoric animal examples include the Mokèlé-Mbèmbé (page 66), Sherman Giant Sloth, and Van Meter Monster.

Cryptid Anatomy

Cryptids are mostly a mix of different animal traits. Here are a few reference pages to help you draw cryptids not included in this book, or to redraw those from the book's tutorials in a new way. From fur types and bodies to paws and tails, try mixing and matching different traits to depict your favorite cryptid or create a new one of your own. For extra practice, you can draw the same cryptid using different references.

Horns

Horns are staples of cryptid anatomy. As many stories and sightings don't specify what type of horn belongs to a cryptid, you can choose to reference whatever you think works best. While there are no rules, artists tend to draw different groups of cryptids with specific types of horns.

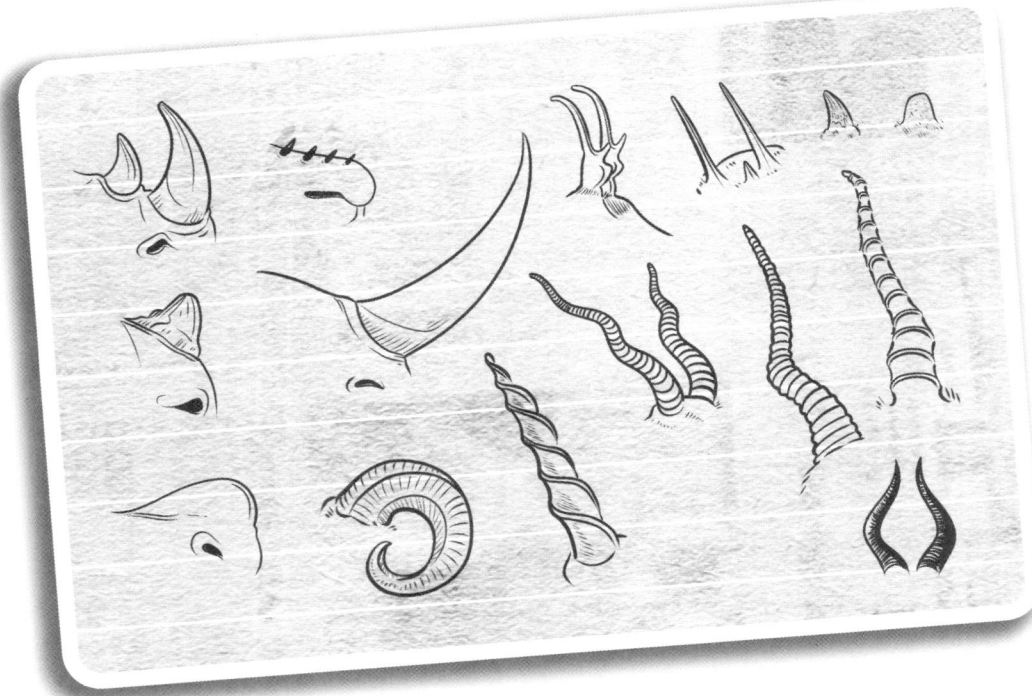

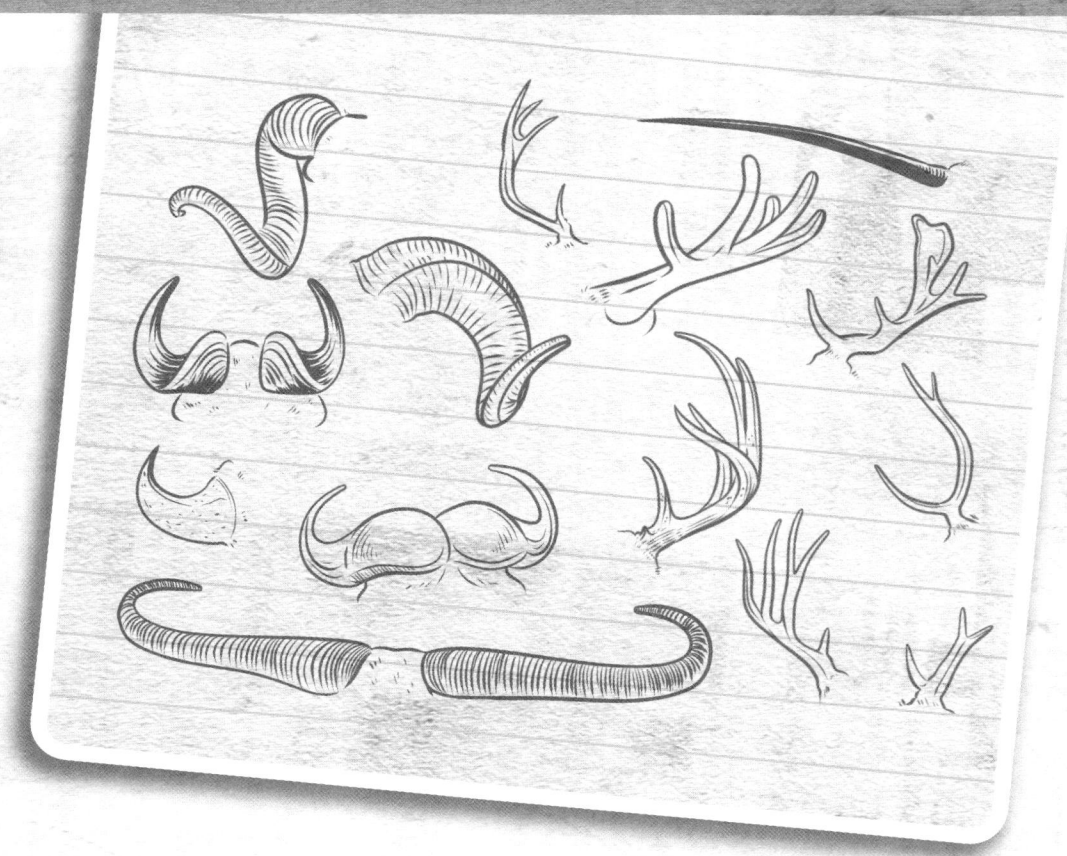

For reptiles, a triangular horn may protrude from the nose, like a rhinoceros. Alternatively, two long, curving horns may jut from the forehead, like an antelope. A dragon may be described as not only having horns on their head and face, but also along their spine and at the end of their tail; these horns may be shorter or thinner. Many useful horned-reptile references can be found in Jurassic- and Cretaceous-era as well as armored dinosaur illustrations.

For threatening, nocturnal monsters, artists often choose sprawling, multipronged antlers to place on their cryptid. Deer horns are often used when drawing horned serpents as well. Antlers come in many shapes, sizes, and textures, so try researching different horned mammals from around the world—or from the Ice Age—to find a perfect reference.

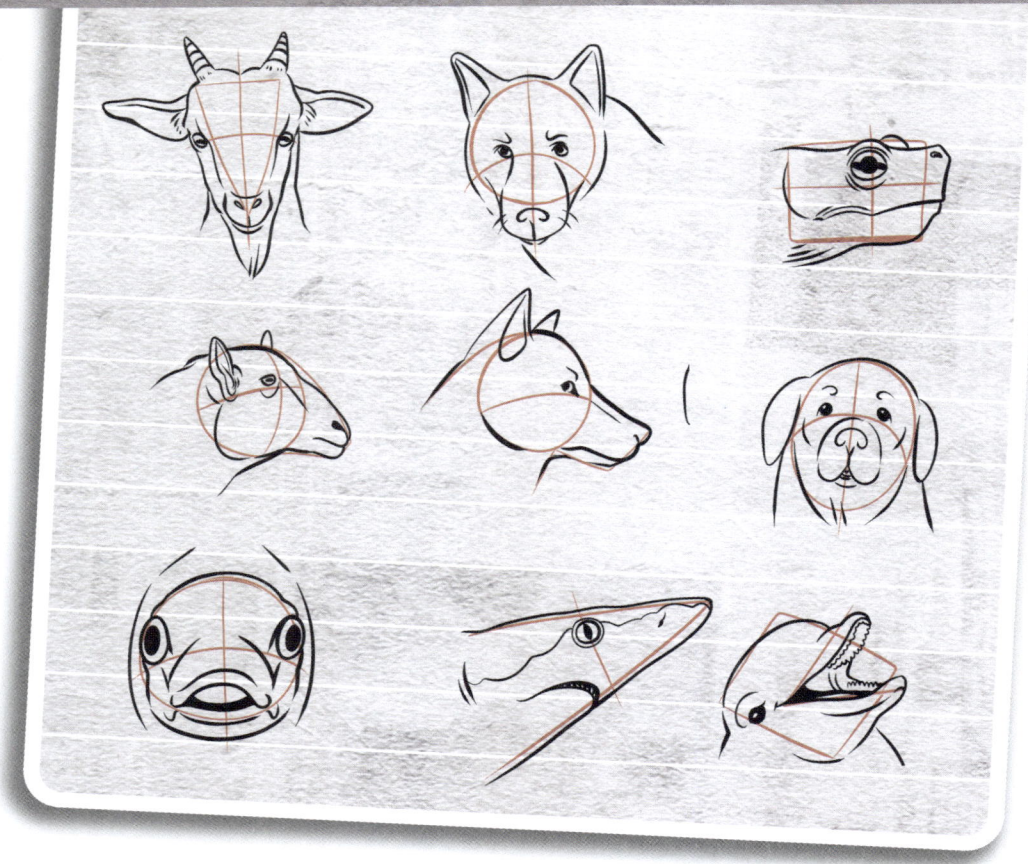

Artists also heavily rely on referencing goats and rams. These horns are generally used on strong or malicious cryptids and positioned above or beside the eyes. Less evil and more mischievous creatures are given the small, round, nub-like horns found on dehorned livestock instead.

Heads

A cryptid's head is more often than not a slightly altered animal's head. When drawing a new cryptid, or making up one of your own, look up several relevant reference heads and practice drawing them. This exercise is also great practice for breaking down images into basic shapes. As you can see in these reference images, most animal heads can be broken down into a circle or oval. Reptiles with thick, bulky heads may be sketched best with a square or rectangle. On the other hand, a triangle may work best for animals like fish or insects.

When a cryptid head requires something a bit more bizarre—such as with aliens or otherworldly entities—insects or deep-sea creatures may give you the inspiration and reference you need.

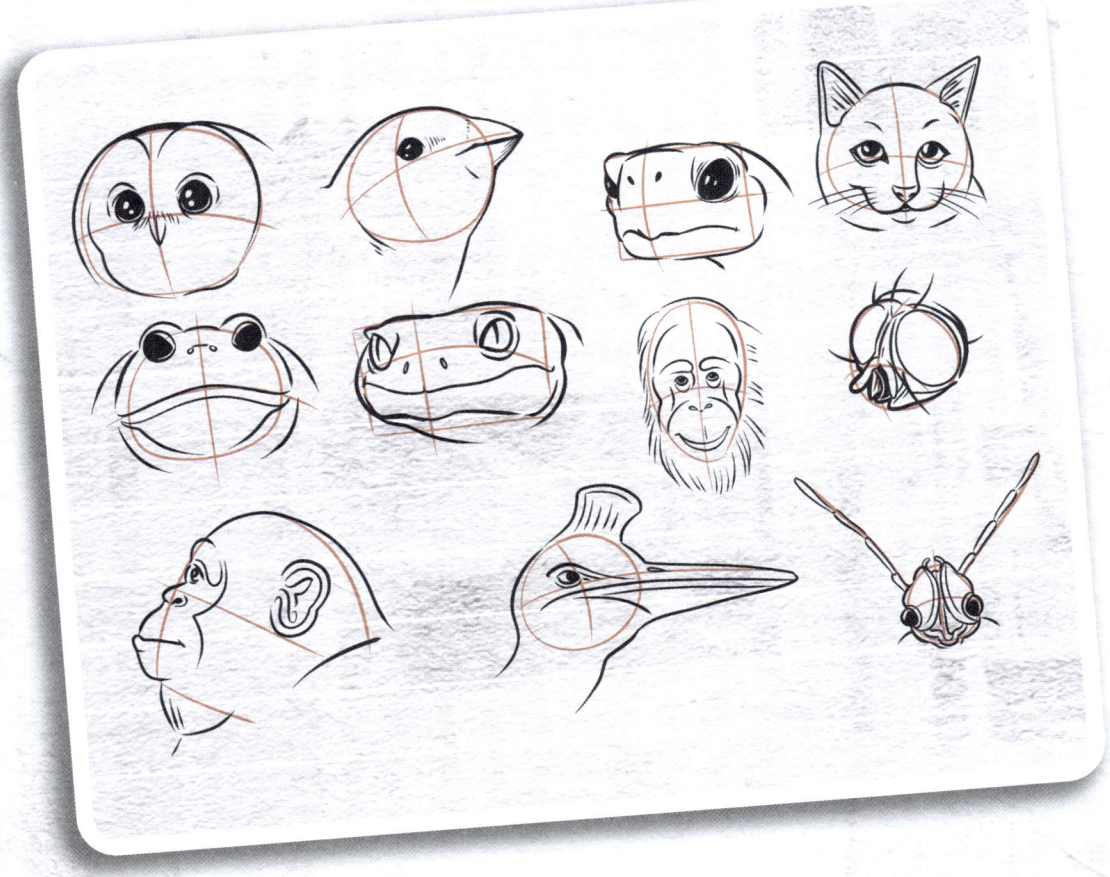

Eyes

Eyes can give a cryptid a lot of personality. When drawing a cryptid, artists usually reference a similar animal or pick something that gives their creature the right feel. Silly or playful cryptids may have large, round eyes. Creepy cryptids may have shiny white pupils, empty sockets, or even a multitude of black specks. Artists generally depict vicious, dangerous cryptids with the horizontal pupils found in goat eyes. Magical or alien cryptids may lack eyes entirely. Pay attention to all the different kinds of eyes found in the animal kingdom; take note of what differentiates one from the other, as well as what qualities they might have.

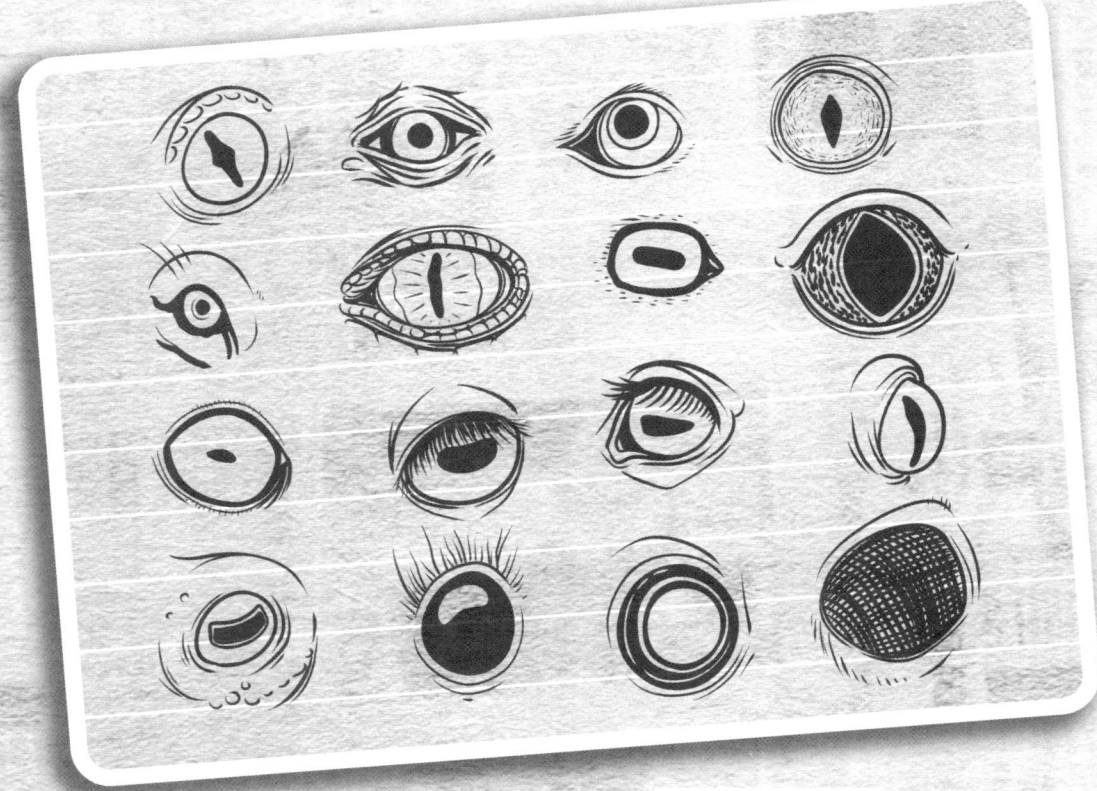

Interested in learning more? Scan the QR code for additional resources.

How to Use This Book

Once you have learned the basics of drawing and cryptids, you'll be ready to tackle all thirty-five of this book's step-by-step cryptid tutorials. Divided into seven sections, each will take you on an adventure into a different habitat and introduce you to the cryptids that call it home. We will begin our journey in the desert, travel up and into the mountains, and then descend into the swamp. Afterward, we will take a swim and explore lakes, rivers, and the ocean. Climbing back to shore, we will wander the woods during the day—and camp overnight to see what lurks after dark. Lastly, we end our expedition among the clouds, flying alongside cryptids and far above all else.

Using everything you've learned, follow each chapter's instructions and draw each cryptid to the best of your ability. Once you've finished your line art, you can try coloring them like I have in my examples, or in your own style. Each chapter will progress in difficulty, beginning with the easiest cryptid to draw from that habitat and ending with the most challenging. Easy drawings rely on one or two basic shapes and cryptids with few details. Advanced tutorials will have more complex sketches and shapes, as well as more details to draw; they may also feature animal types that are slightly challenging to work with. While some tutorials are more complicated than others, you should still be able to flip to any page and understand how to draw each creature. Whether you'd like to tackle every cryptid in order or start with your favorites, remember that if you practice and take your time, you can draw anything!

Creature Key

DESERT-PROWLING CRYPTIDS

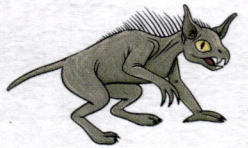

Chupacabra
First sighted in Puerto Rico, this cryptid feeds on animals by sucking their blood.

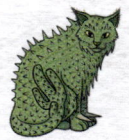

Cactus Cat
A thorny cat that hails from the American Southwest and has a branched tail that resembles a cactus.

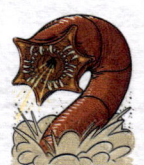

Mongolian Death Worm
This worm prefers to stay underground beneath the dunes of the Gobi Desert.

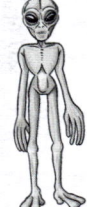

Roswell Alien
Landing in Roswell, New Mexico, this otherworldly visitor comes in peace.

MOUNTAIN-TREKKING CRYPTIDS

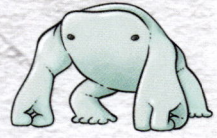

Grafton Monster
This blobby white cryptid has no head and resides in the Appalachian Mountains of West Virginia.

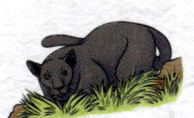

Blue Mountains Panther
A big cat that reportedly roams the Blue Mountains near Sydney, Australia.

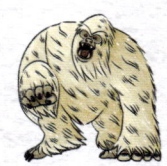

Yeti
Also known as the Abominable Snowman, this cryptid prefers to keep to itself.

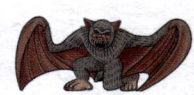

Ahool
A winged cryptid that lives high up in the trees of Indonesia's rainforests.

SWAMP-LURKING CRYPTIDS

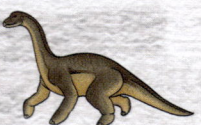

Mokèlé-Mbèmbé
In the Congo River Basin resides a creature that looks like a type of dinosaur.

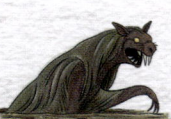

Bunyip
This cryptid from Australian Aboriginal folklore can be found in swamps and billabongs.

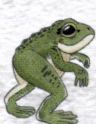

Loveland Frogman
A froglike cryptid that was first spotted in the town of Loveland, Ohio.

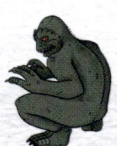

Lizardman of Scape Ore Swamp
Sightings in the 1980s of a lizard-like cryptid nearby Scape Ore Swamp in South Carolina gave rise to the legend of the Lizardman.

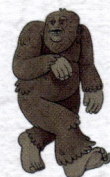

Sasquatch
Also known as Bigfoot, this iconic cryptid is from the forests of the Pacific Northwest region of North America.

WATER-DWELLING CRYPTIDS

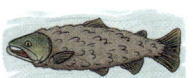

Fur-Bearing Trout
From North American folklore, this fish has fur to weather the frosty winters.

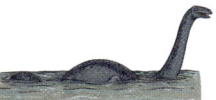

Loch Ness Monster
An iconic sea monster said to lurk the depths of Loch Ness in Scotland.

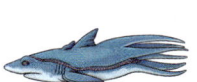

Lusca
This cryptid from Caribbean folklore enjoys basking in the warm waters of the Bahamas.

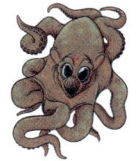

Kraken
Sightings of giant squid in the cold waters near Norway and Iceland may have provided the origins of this legendary beast.

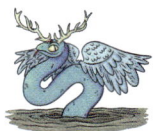

Uktena
Also called the Horned Serpent, this mythological creature appears throughout the Indigenous folklore of North America.

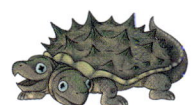

Ogua
It is said that a giant turtle with two heads lives in the rivers of Appalachia.

FOREST-CREEPING CRYPTIDS

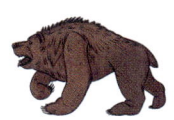

Nandi Bear
A highly dangerous predator that is found in western Kenya.

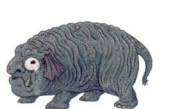

Squonk
Brooding in the hemlock forests of Pennsylvania, this cryptid has very low self-esteem.

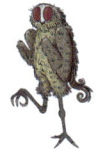

Chickcharney
A flightless bird from the Bahamas that is said to bring good luck to those who treat it well.

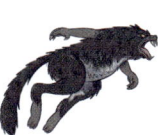

Devil Monkey
This cryptid has been sighted throughout the United States and Canada and is described as looking like a baboon.

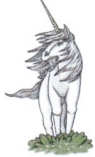

Unicorn
Often depicted as a white horse with a horn that sticks out from the middle of its head.

NIGHT-SEEKING CRYPTIDS

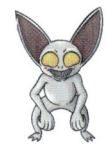

Hopkinsville Goblin
An alien that appeared one night near the city of Hopkinsville, Kentucky.

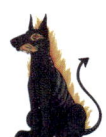

Hellhound
A mythological dog said to guard the underworld.

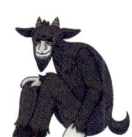

Kentucky Goatman
Half-goat, half-man, all menace.

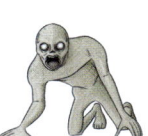

Pale Crawler
A humanoid figure that emerges at night, crawling in search of food.

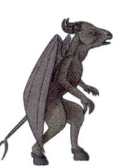

Jersey Devil
The cursed thirteenth child of Mother Leeds from New Jersey.

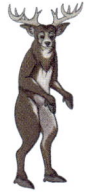

Not-Deer
A cryptid from Appalachian folklore that is very similar to a deer, but just *isn't*.

HIGH-FLYING CRYPTIDS

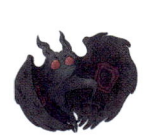

Mothman
This winged cryptid may have been a portent of warning to the inhabitants in the town of Point Pleasant, West Virginia.

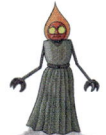

Flatwoods Monster
An extraterrestrial figure that first terrified witnesses in the town of Flatwoods, West Virginia, in 1952.

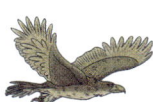

Thunderbird
From North American Indigenous mythology comes this enormous bird that can create thunder by flapping its wings.

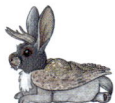

Wolpertinger
A hybrid animal that makes its home in the alpine forests of Southern Germany.

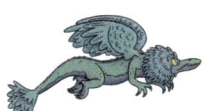

Snallygaster
This chimera was first talked about by German immigrants living near Maryland and Washington, DC.

DESERT-PROWLING

CRYPTIDS

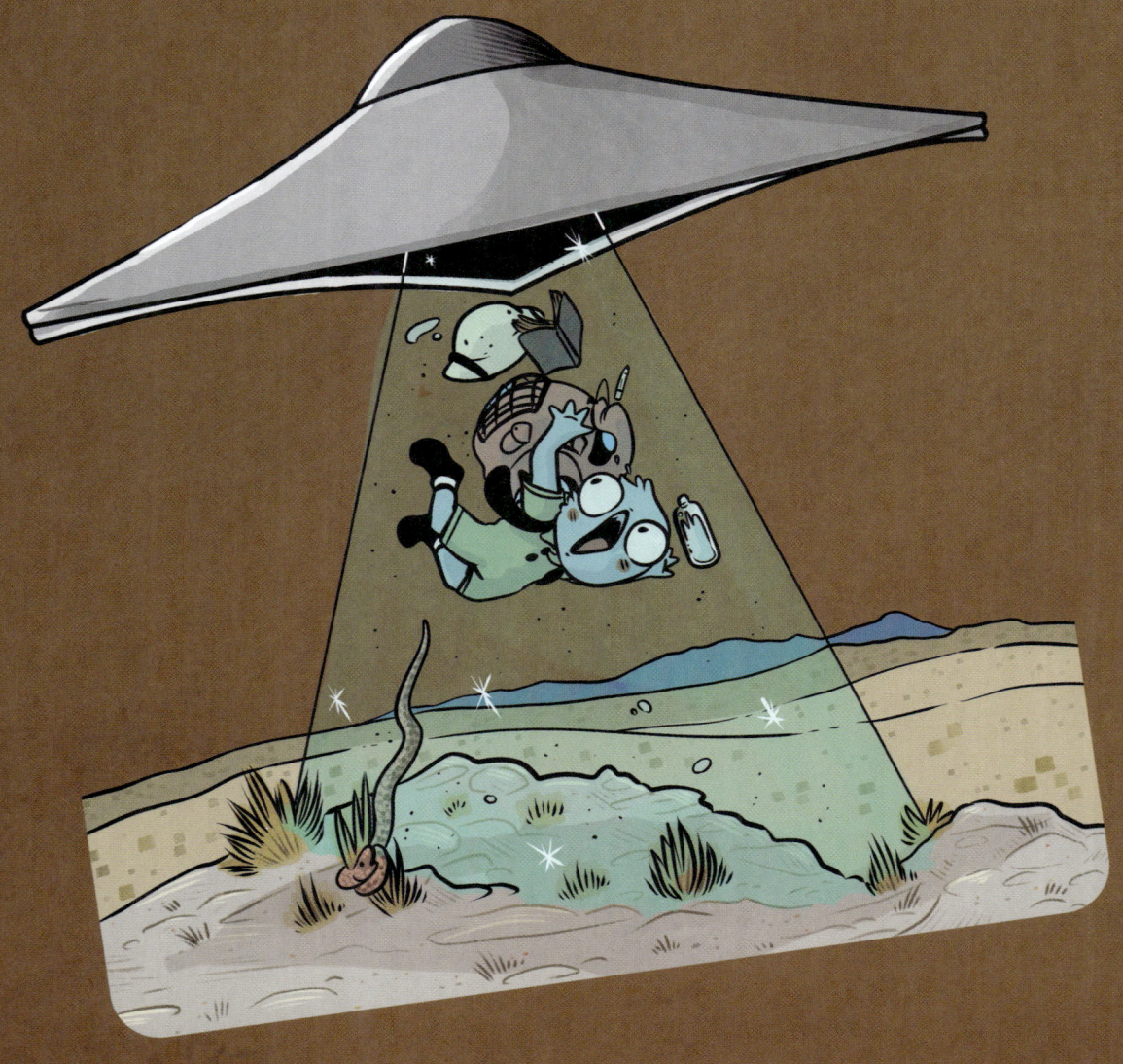

Vast regions that receive little water, deserts are extreme environments with harsh conditions. From stretches of flat rock to sandy dunes or empty expanses of ice, deserts can be hot or cold, and few trees exist. Animals here have exceptional adaptations to survive their intense worlds—and so do desert cryptids, usually possessing tough skin, sharp spikes, and a vicious disposition. Clear, empty skies and open landscapes beckon cryptid visitors as well; entities from outer space are encountered in the desert more than any other biome.

Chupacabra

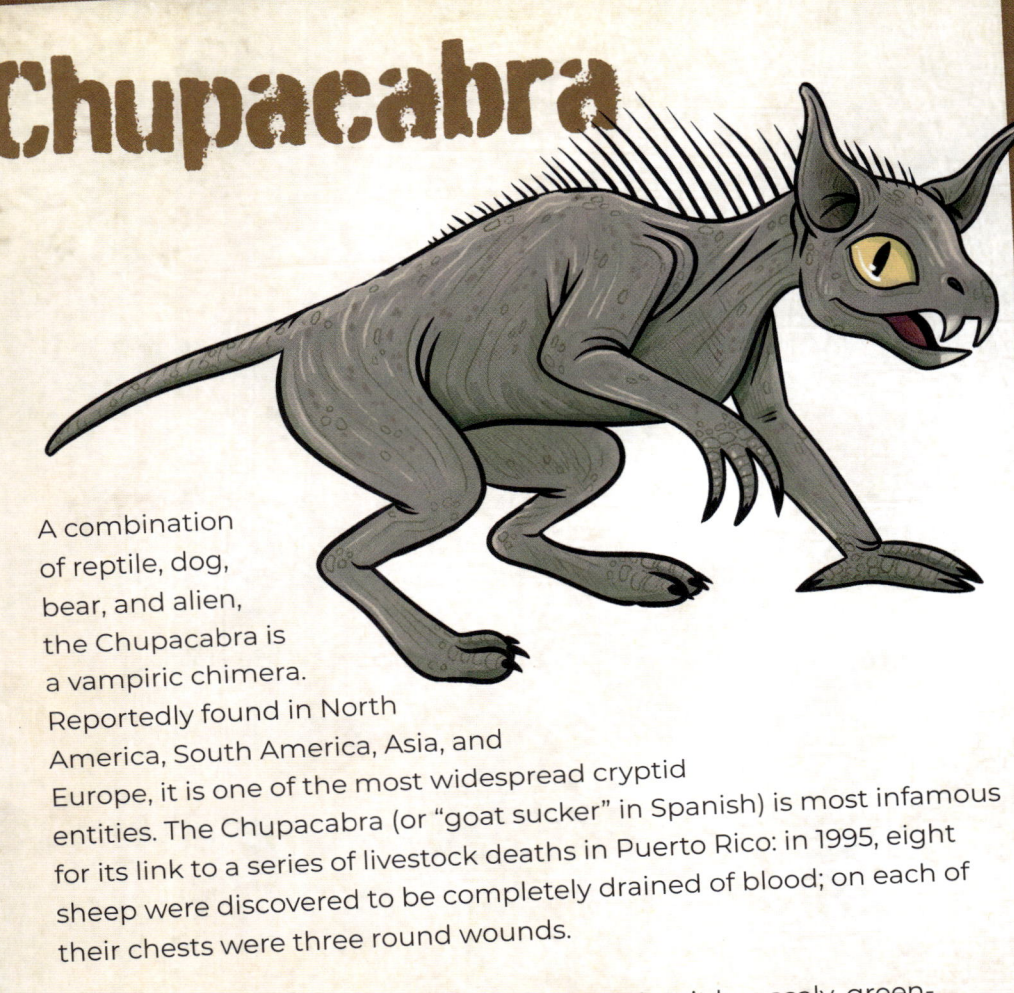

A combination of reptile, dog, bear, and alien, the Chupacabra is a vampiric chimera. Reportedly found in North America, South America, Asia, and Europe, it is one of the most widespread cryptid entities. The Chupacabra (or "goat sucker" in Spanish) is most infamous for its link to a series of livestock deaths in Puerto Rico: in 1995, eight sheep were discovered to be completely drained of blood; on each of their chests were three round wounds.

Most descriptions of the Chupacabra note that it has scaly, green-gray skin and quills on its back. Between three and four feet (1 m) tall, early stories describe it as hopping like a kangaroo. The second most common description compares it to a hairless, bony coyote. Cryptozoologists claim the creature is a mutated canine, whereas ufologists explain it as an extraterrestrial experiment.

Sketch a circle; inside, sketch a downward angled, slightly curving horizontal guideline. On top of your circle and to the left, sketch a downward sloping, curving line.

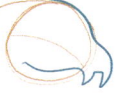

Following your circle, draw the top of the head. The Chupacabra's snout will poke from the bottom right of the circle. Below, add two fangs and a smile.

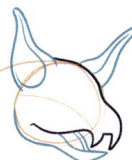

On top of the head, draw two pointed ears. They are somewhat teardrop shaped, but curvier. Next, draw the lower jaw. Using your sketch, follow the circle, then angle outward. Add one big fang that almost touches the other teeth.

Using your guideline, draw a large eye in the middle of your circle. Within, draw a sharp pupil. On the snout, add a nostril.

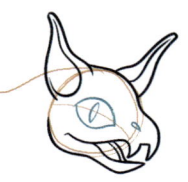

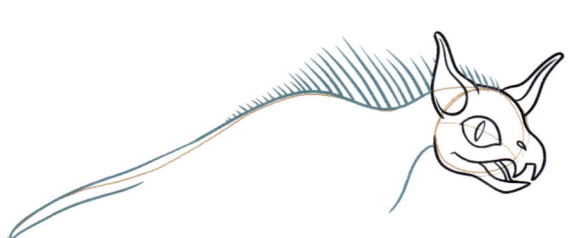

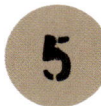

Following your sketch, draw the Chupacabra's back and tail. Afterward, add its spines. These will grow in length until reaching the neck; from there, they decrease in height. Each spine curves slightly backward; you can draw them at different angles instead to make your creature spookier. Lastly, draw the neck below.

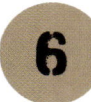

Draw the first part of the front arms. In this example, the Chupacabra has one arm on the ground and one raised. Finish the arms and add three clawed hands under each one. The hand on the left pauses in the air, whereas the right holds itself up and is pressed against the ground.

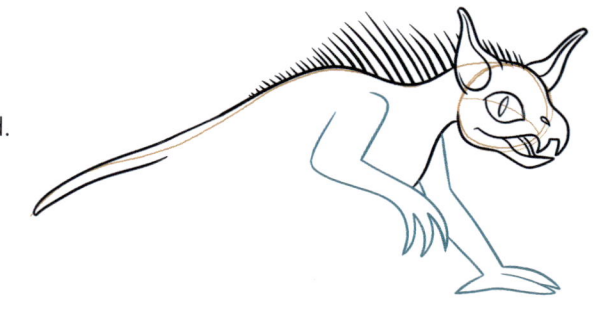

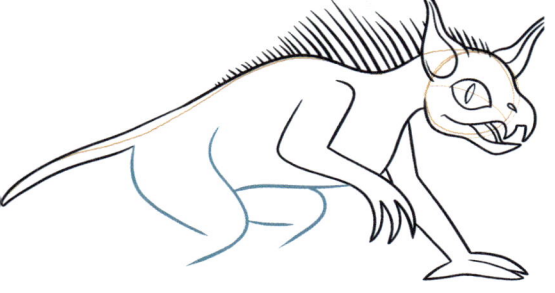

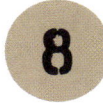

7 Next, draw the stomach. Afterward, draw the top of its back legs. The right leg will be partially obscured and a little smaller.

8 Connected to Step 7's lines, draw doglike feet. These limbs have upraised ankles attached to long soles and rounded paws.

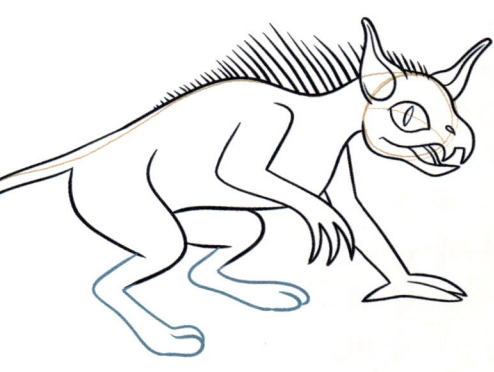

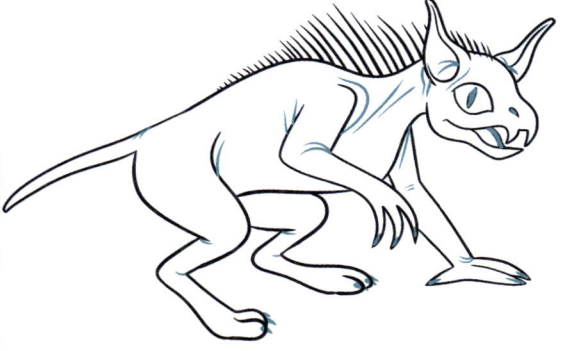

9 Erase your sketch lines. The Chupacabra is a rough-skinned, wrinkly creature. Where the body bends, add a curve or two to show the skin's texture. Afterward, color in the pupil, nostril, back lip, and claws.

Cactus Cat

The Cactus Cat is a fearsome critter from United States folklore (California, Colorado, Nevada, and New Mexico). Created by cowboys and frontiersmen, tales of this cryptid were intended to frighten those unfamiliar with the American Southwest and its environment, making it seem like a more dangerous place than it already was. Covered in needlelike fur, the Cactus Cat greatly resembles a bobcat, but with a branched tail like a saguaro cactus and dagger-like horns on their front legs.

At night, the Cactus Cat comes out from hiding to feed. Slashing open cacti with their arms, they drink the sap found within. While they are herbivorous, that doesn't mean they aren't dangerous. Travelers passing by their dens or near cacti at night may be attacked by their spiny tails and arms.

Sketch a circle; inside, sketch a vertical and a slightly curved horizontal guideline. Next, to the left, sketch a curve that transitions to a nearly vertical line at its end.

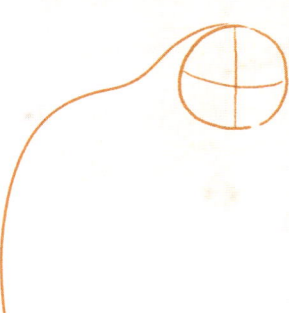

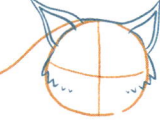

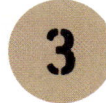

Using your circle as a guide, draw two triangular ears on each side of the head. Afterward, draw the inner ears and the top of the head. Below each ear, draw the Cat's spiky cheeks.

Using your guidelines, draw two eyes in the center of your circle; the eyes should barely dip below your horizontal guideline. In the middle of each eye, draw a sharp pupil. Above each eye, draw three spikes; these are the animal's pointy eyebrows. Next, draw the Cat's nose, which is like a squashed heart with a line down its center. Afterward, give the Cat a smug smile and a chin below.

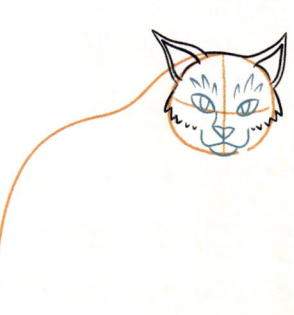

Sketch the rest of the cat's body. Begin with its chest, then add the front legs, paws, and tail.

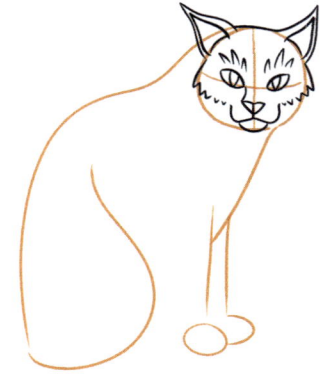

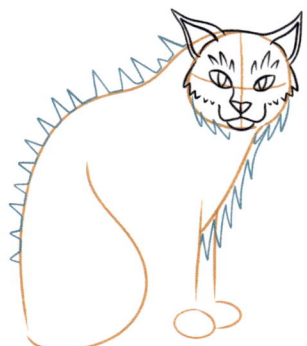

Draw spiky fur at the bottom of each side of the Cat's head. Use your circle to keep the formation following a rounded curve. Leave the space below the chin empty. Under the head, draw more spiky fur down the neck, pausing at the front legs. Then, draw a row of thicker spines that follow the curve of the Cat's back. Unlike in the previous steps, these spikes have gaps between them that are connected by lines.

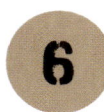

Next, draw the base of the cat's tail using your sketch as a guide. Now finish the tail. Draw a few cactus branches, which can be broken down into four rectangular shapes. Sketch their placement before drawing them. Like rounded boxes that curve into the main branch, the tail is similar in shape to a pitchfork with an extra box at its base.

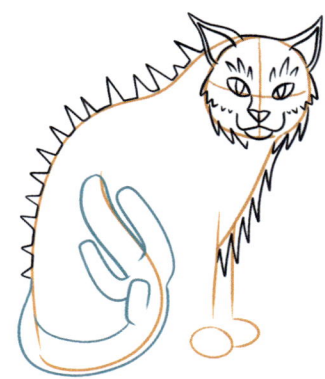

TIP

The Cactus Cat's tail is topped by a cactus. In this example, we use a saguaro cactus, but you can model your cat's tail of any cactus you like.

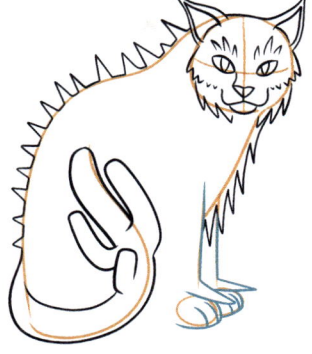

Use straight lines to draw the front of the Cat's arms. Before you reach each paw, draw a long spike pointing away from the animal; these are its cactus-cutting daggers. Underneath, add its paws.

8

Before we can finish the foreleg, we have to draw the hind leg. Near the top of the tail, draw a swooping, zigzagging line. Make sure the back leg connects to the tail. Afterward, finish drawing the front paw, then the back foot.

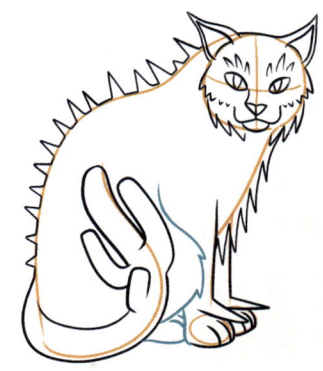

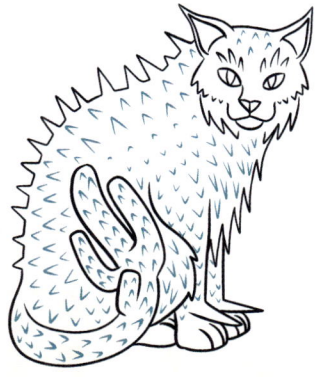

Erase your sketch lines. Lastly, add texture to the animal. A Cactus Cat's fur is comprised of cactus spines. In the example, we use a V shape of varying sizes and angles to show how the thorns lay on the body. The thorns are more prominent on the animal's back and longer and thinner on its chest.

Mongolian Death Worm

Known locally as Olgoi-Khorkhoi, the Mongolian Death Worm slithers below the dunes of the Gobi Desert and hunts humans in its territory. Red, tubular, and sausage-like, its local name translates to "large-intestine worm." It has been reported to be as small as two feet (61 cm) long and as large as seven feet (2 m). Having few discernible features, it only opens its wide, toothy, circular mouth after fully emerging from its burrow.

The Death Worm can spew a yellow, corrosive substance at its prey from a long distance, and, in some accounts, stun targets with electricity. Luckily, folklore states that the creature rarely comes to the surface. Arising after rain or from hunger, a traveling Death Worm can be detected by the quivering waves of sand it moves in its wake.

First, sketch a circle. This cryptid is tall and will wind to the right, so make sure you have enough space to draw it.

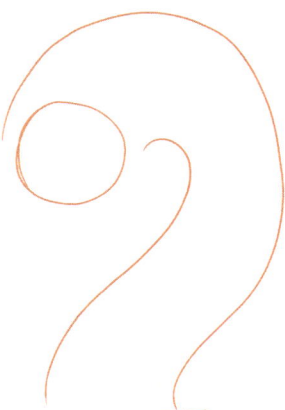

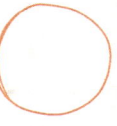

Next, sketch the worm's body. Death Worms are tubelike monsters; sketch a tall, back-and-forth curve to show its slithery form. Next, sketch a horizontal line at the base of your sketch to show where the ground begins.

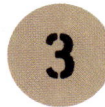

The Death Worm's mouth opens into six triangular flaps of skin. Using your circle as a guide, sketch each flap around the head; by the end, it will look a little like a drawing of the sun.

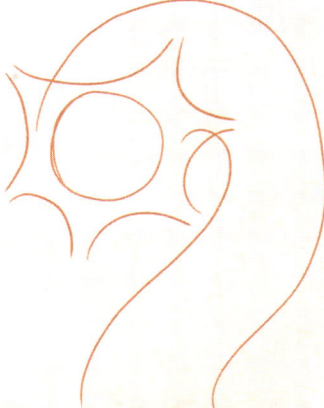

4

Draw around Step 3's sketches. Instead of meeting at a sharp point, your lines should round the sketches' gaps. Then, draw three long, sharp, curving fangs inside each mouth flap. The teeth should point toward the center of the mouth.

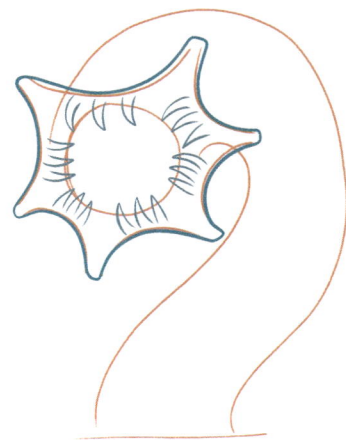

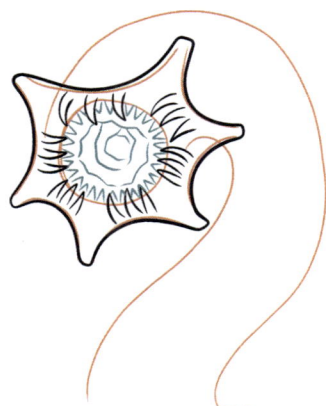

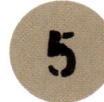

5

Using your circle as a guide, draw another row of smaller fangs. Each tooth should point toward the mouth's center. Step 5's fangs will obscure some teeth; make sure to draw only the parts that would be visible. Once all teeth are in place, draw the inside of the worm's throat. Overlap and shorten your lines with each layer.

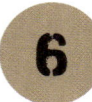

6

Add some fleshy texture to the creature's mouth and color in the deepest portion of its throat.

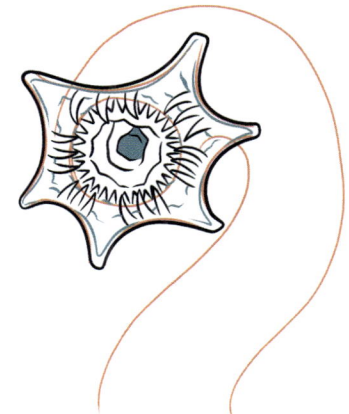

FUN FACT

Some people believe that Mongolian Death Worm sightings are a misidentification of the Tartar sand boa. This snake sometimes hides under the sand and can grow up to four feet (1 m) long.

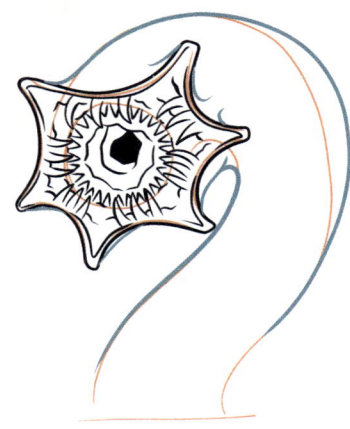

7

Extending from the top left mouth flap, draw the Death Worm's back. However, don't draw your line all the way to the ground. We will use that space in Step 9. Now, draw six lines from five of the mouth flaps; these lines should curve and stretch toward the creature's body. Then, draw the Death Worm's belly. Leave space at the bottom.

8

Erase your sketch lines. A giant worm exploding out of the sand makes a mess. Draw clouds of dust, waves of sand, and airborne particulates at the base of the creature.

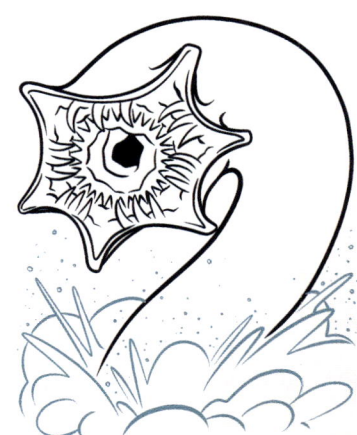

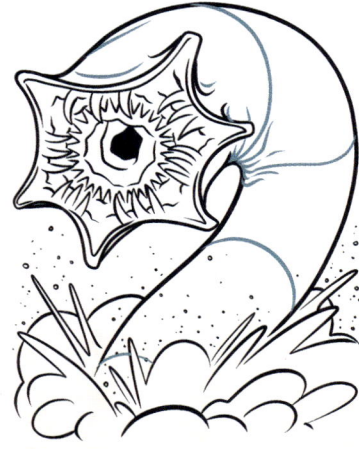

9

Lastly, add some texture to the Mongolian Death Worm's body. Like a segmented earthworm, draw a line from one side of the creature to the other, four times. Then, add curvy lines to show where its skin bunches up or stretches.

Roswell Alien

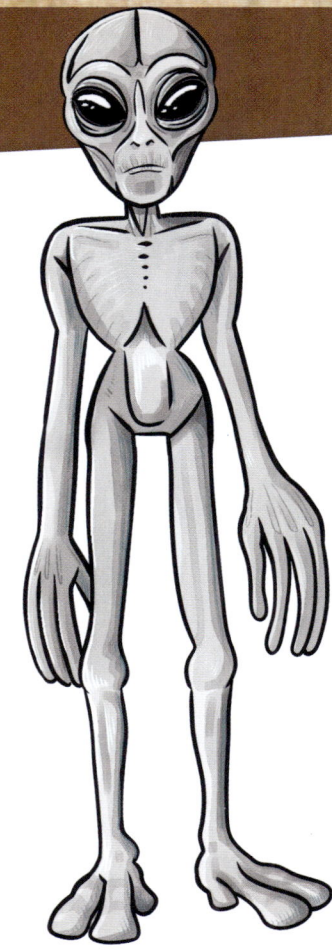

It was in Roswell, New Mexico, United States, when something fell from the sky in 1947 in the middle of the Chihuahuan Desert. Crashing to the ground, this "something" exploded in a jumble of metallic scraps, foil, and other reflective material. Was it a weather balloon, as the local air force stated, or was it a spaceship from outer space? Since the Roswell Incident, additional UFO sightings and close encounters have occurred in the area. Ufologists and alien enthusiasts flock to the region to hunt for UFO debris, peer at Area 51 (where the remains of the "spaceship" were said to be taken), and watch the skies.

The events at Roswell have influenced and shaped our understanding of aliens and what they look like, including the classic tall, bug-eyed, humanoid depiction here.

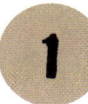

1

Sketch a base for your alien. Start by sketching a circle. Near the bottom of your circle, sketch a curved, horizontal line. Next, sketch an extended vertical line down the shape. Then, sketch a rectangle; leave a gap between the two shapes.

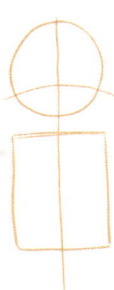

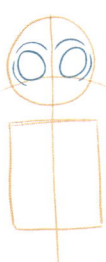

2

Draw the alien's eyes, which look like egg-shaped ovals. Use your horizontal guideline to place them on the face. Next, add a round curve above and on the outer edge of the eye.

3

Using your circle as a guide, draw the top of the head. Then, draw another, more dramatically curved line under the eyes. The alien has a long face shaped like an upside-down teardrop.

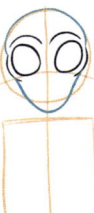

FUN FACT

Roswell is so well known for its alien encounter that it has its own UFO museum and research center. Many of the businesses in the town are also alien themed.

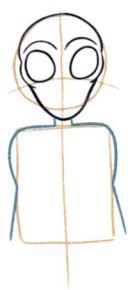

Below the chin, draw the neck. Follow your rectangle and draw the alien's shoulders.

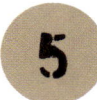

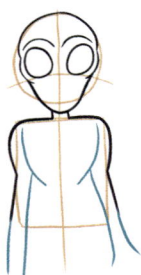

Draw the alien's chest. Its curved lines should reach just below the box's center and nearly touch your vertical guideline. Where the shoulders dip inward, draw two vertical lines from the chest. They should reach past your rectangle and stop at the bottom of your guideline. Next, extend the arm lines from Step 4.

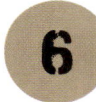

Below the chest, draw the alien's waist, which curves to the bottom of the box. Then, draw the outer legs. At the base of your rectangle, mirror these lines to draw the inner legs; as you draw these lines, taper the leg's shape. Connect the legs with a line, following the sketch. Lastly, add knees to each leg. Leave a gap at the bottom of each leg for Step 7.

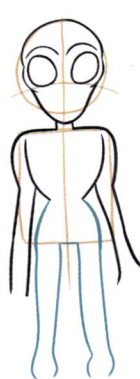

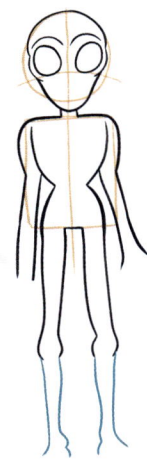

7

Draw the lower legs. At the bottom of the leg, add a bumpy ankle.

8

Draw the Roswell Alien's hands and its long and lumpy fingers. The left hand is partially concealed behind the left leg. Then, draw the feet. Unlike the hands, the feet are made up of three broad, flat appendages. The big toe is a third of the size of the other two toes.

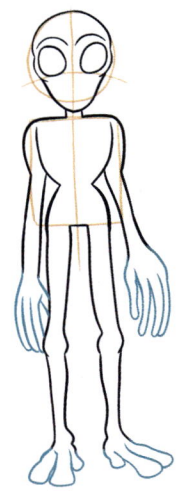

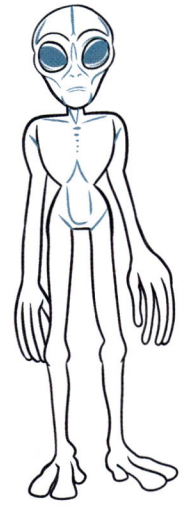

9

Erase your sketch lines. Now, add some details. Color in the alien's eyes; leave a wedge above and below the shape uncolored to make eyelids. Eye creases give the creature an inquisitive look. Add wrinkles to the forehead and the alien's nose. Draw its cheeks and mouth. The Roswell Alien's skin is pulled tight across its skeleton. Add a few lines on the chest, shoulders, and neck to make this more apparent. Draw the stomach and waistlines.

MOUNTAIN-TREKKING

CRYPTIDS

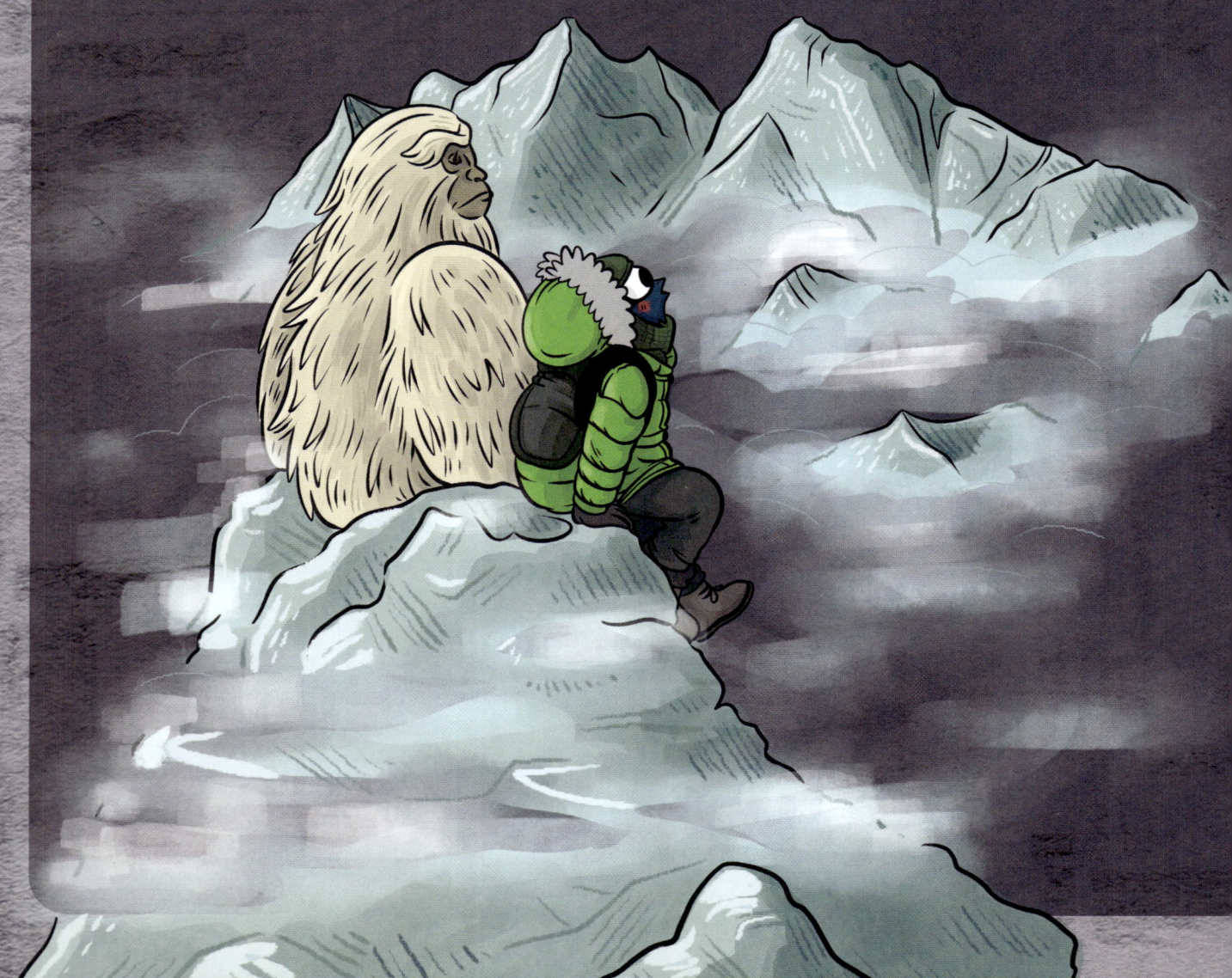

Montane ecosystems are diverse. Some mountains host humid rainforests with dense forests that are hard to navigate; others are dry, rocky, and incredibly cold. As mountain ranges are challenging to explore and usually remote, it should be no surprise that many cryptids are said to hide within them. Some of the most famous, like the Yeti, live in the highest, harshest portions of the mountain. Most, however, live below the tree line and in less intense circumstances.

Grafton Monster

First spotted in 1964 in Tygart Country, West Virginia, United States, the Grafton Monster is a bright white blobby creature that appears headless. Journalist Robert Cockrell was the first to observe and document the cryptid, writing an article about it in the *Grafton Sentinel*. The newspaper's coverage generated a monster hunt throughout the Appalachian Mountains. While cryptid hunters claimed to see the creature and hear an unsettling, deep bellow, no physical evidence was ever recovered.

Witnesses have described the Grafton Monster as having seallike skin, a wide, misshapen head close to its chest, and a height of seven to nine feet (2 to 3 m). Some ufologists believe it is an extraterrestrial visitor. Cryptozoologists argue instead that it is an underground entity or a bigfoot with albinism.

Sketch a rectangle. Below its center, sketch a horizontal guideline.

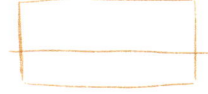

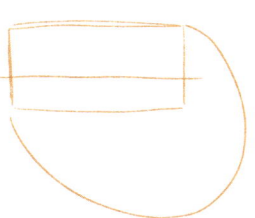

From the bottom left corner to the top right corner of your rectangle, sketch a curving arch.

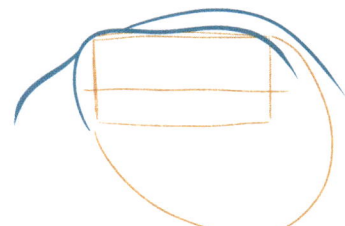

Draw the head. Use your sketch as a guide to draw a curving line from the bottom left corner of your rectangle to the top right; this line dips down in the center of the box. Do not draw it past the height of your horizontal guideline. Then, add the shoulders. To the left, draw a short, downward sloping curve. Nearby, draw an arch to the right that curves past and below Step 3's line.

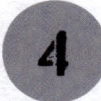

4

Draw the arms with two long, wobbly, vertical lines that curl to the right at their ends. Then, use your sketch as a guide to draw the chest and belly; there will be a gap between the head and chest, as well as between the chest and belly.

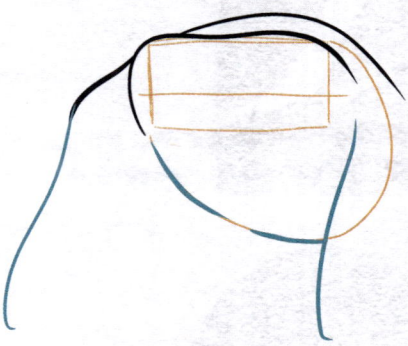

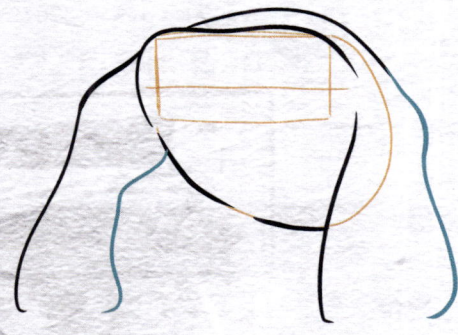

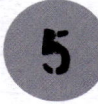

5

Draw the rest of the cryptid's strong, bulky arms. Each limb is thick and lumpy.

6

Between the creature's two arms, draw the left leg. Next to the right arm, draw the cryptid's lower back and right leg.

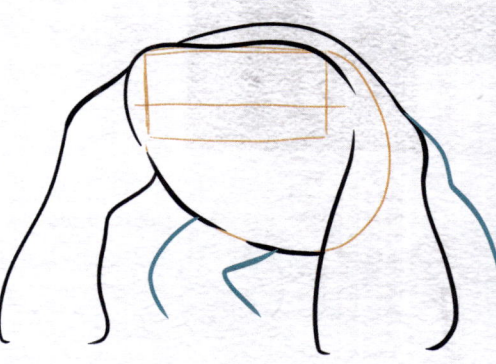

FUN FACT

In the days following the Grafton Monster's initial sighting, hikers and monster hunters reported not only hearing bellowing from the woods but also an eerie whistling near the local river. By the next week, both sounds disappeared.

7

At the end of each arm, draw three thick, blocky fingers. On the left arm, the thumb and forefinger face each other and slightly overlap; the third finger is barely seen behind them. On the right arm, draw two big, rectangular fingers on the left side of the hand and a curled thumb to the right.

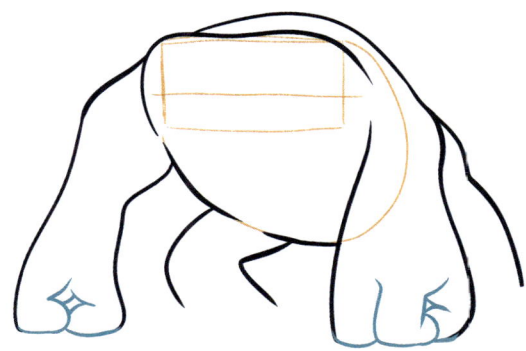

8

Draw the feet. At the end of each leg, draw a series of squashed, round curves. While the left foot has four visible toes, the right foot only has three. On the left foot, draw a thumb-like toe that points to the right.

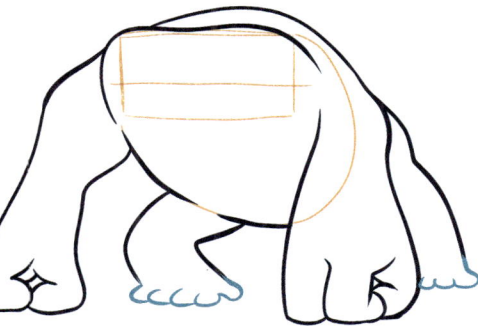
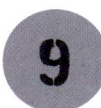

9

Erase your sketch lines and add a few last details. On each side of the head, draw two oval eyes. Add a few marks and curves where the body bends. These marks also help show how gelatinous and bubbly it is.

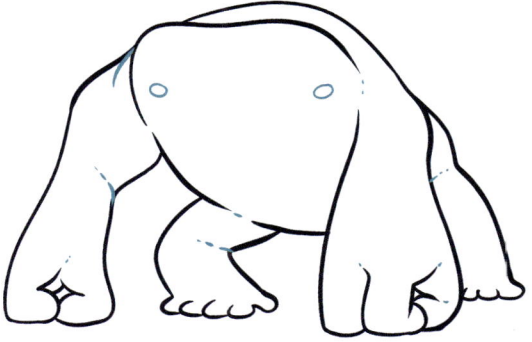

Blue Mountains Panther

West of Sydney, Australia, lurks a large cat. Described as a black panther, the animal was first reported in the wild in the early 1900s—and reports have only increased since then. Called the Blue Mountains Panther or Lithgow Panther, this cryptid has hundreds of documented accounts, which have encouraged theories on the animal's origins in the area. Escaped circus animals, lost World War II United States military mascots, and released illegal pets are a few speculations on how they have turned up in Sydney. Though unconvincing evidence to some, dead livestock and strange scratch marks are proof enough for many locals that something unusual is out there. The Australian government took these panther sightings seriously; several investigations were conducted from 1999 to 2013.

Alien Big Cats (also known as phantom cats) are a worldwide cryptid phenomenon. Large felines encountered in an area where they don't belong are not uncommon.

1

Sketch a tilted, downward pointing triangle. Add a slanted guideline down its center.

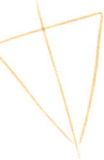

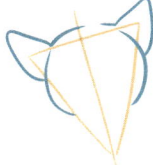

2

On the top two points of your triangle, draw a round, triangular ear. Near the top of the ears, draw a round, outward curving line on each side of the head. Then, draw the top of the head, leaving a gap on the right side.

3

Next, draw the inner ears and their fluffy fur. Where the cheeks end, draw a rounded W, joining each side of the head together. Above, draw and color in the feline's nose; the triangle's top line should curve downward at this angle. Add a few whiskers on each side of the mouth.

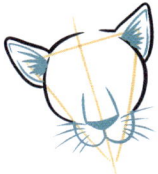

TIP

Reference images of the Blue Mountains to draw a different landscape under your cryptid! What plants are found in the area? What are the rocks like? Large felines such as this one are cryptids in many other countries too. Try putting your cat in an entirely different environment for something new.

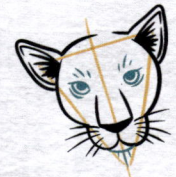

4

Draw the cat's chin and add a few whiskers to it. Above the nose, on each side of the snout, draw a sharp eye; the upper eyelid should extend a little farther outward than the bottom eyelid. Above each eye, draw three eyebrow hairs. Below the eyes, draw an eyelid.

5

Draw the back. First, draw a curve that stems from between the left ear and head; swoop upward at the end of it. Next to it, draw another rounded curve.

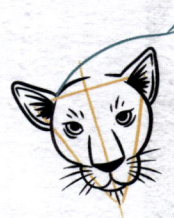

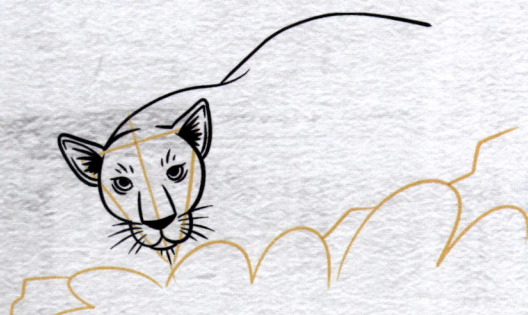

6

Sketch the foliage the animal is lurking through. From left to right, at an upward-slanted angle, sketch overlapping round curves and square shapes. These forms will become spiky grasses and rocks.

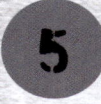

7

Using your sketch as a guide, draw the ground around the cat. For grass, use triangular lines, sharp angles, and long, gentle curves of varying lengths. For rocks, draw long, blocky lines that waver and dip at angles.

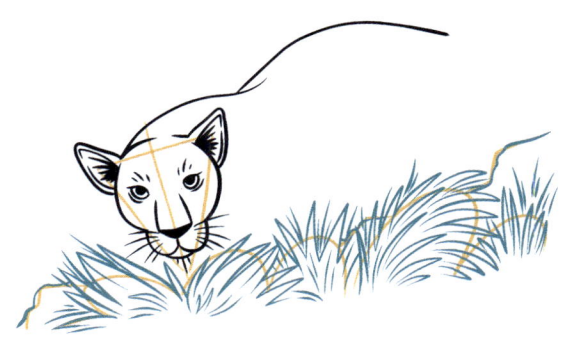

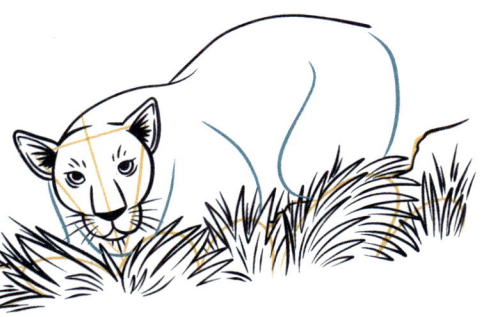

8

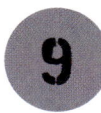

Between the lines of the cat and ground, add the arms and legs. As the animal is hunkered down, we won't need to draw its lower limbs at all—only the curves of its shoulders, chest, thigh, and rump. Leave a gap between the back and thigh of the animal for a tail in Step 9. Make sure not to draw through your plants!

9

Erase your sketch lines. Then, add the tail. Extending from the back, it curls behind the animal and reappears above the head. Sketch the tail before drawing it if you need to.

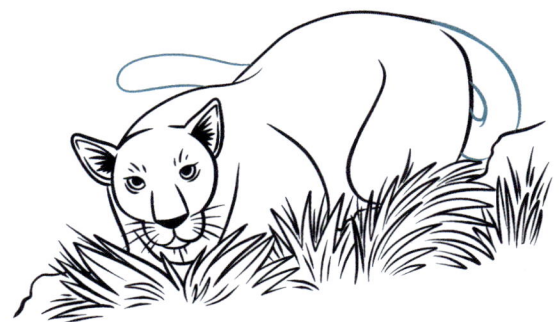

Yeti

Roaming the slopes and high elevations of the Himalayan Mountains, the Yeti (or Abominable Snowman) is a large, bipedal, apelike entity. Like Sasquatch (page 82), it has been the focus of many monster hunts and cryptozoological expeditions. A collection of video footage, audio recordings, footprint plaster casts, and photographs of the Yeti allegedly exist.

According to local folklore, there are three types of Yetis, easily distinguishable by their fur color or height. The most aggressive kind is also the largest; it has black fur and stands up to fifteen feet (5 m) tall. A type found higher in the mountains has a variety of hair colors but only the third and smallest has red hair and grows up to 5 feet (1.5 m) tall. These are not the only descriptions of Yetis, though, with more accounts from Bhutan, China, India, Nepal, and Siberia.

1

Sketch a thin oval that is tilted to the right. In its center, sketch a downward curving horizontal guideline and a diagonal guideline. Around the oval, sketch a wide, rounded triangle; the top of the shape should graze your oval.

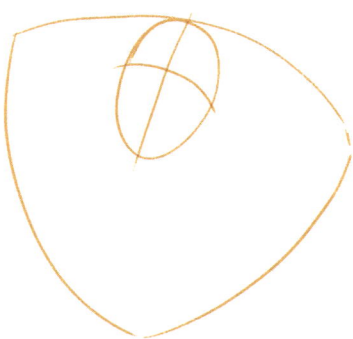

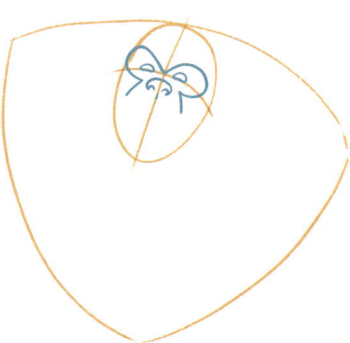

2

Using your guidelines, draw the Yeti's face. Start with the eyes and add two oval, bean-like shapes on your horizontal guideline. Below, draw a round nose and a dash. Next, like a butterfly wing, draw two arches around the eyes.

TIP

Yetis come in different sizes, furry coats, and temperaments! Try redrawing this tutorial based on other Yeti descriptions, using different face types and expressions, or altering the creature's height or bulk.

3

Connected to Step 2's lines, draw the mouth. Inside, add a wide fang on each side of the upper lip. Between the large teeth, draw four smaller, triangular fangs. Below, draw two larger fangs on each side of the mouth that are double the length of the top teeth and curve slightly inward. Just like on top, draw four small teeth between the bottom fangs.

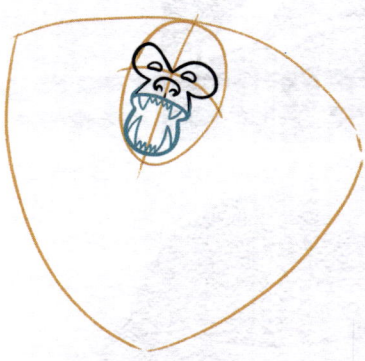

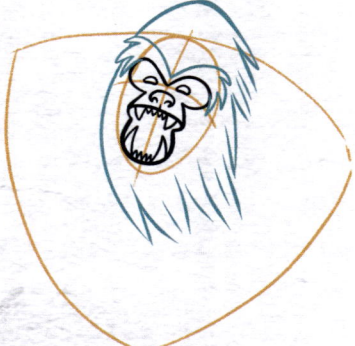

4

Copying the curve around the Yeti's eyes, give the creature a bushy unibrow. Use your oval as a guide to draw the top of its cone-shaped head and its left side. Add sharp wedges and curved lines below and to the right of the oval; this gives the cryptid a furry appearance and shows its beard blowing in the wind.

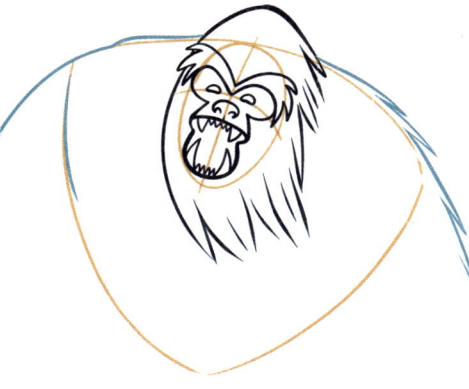
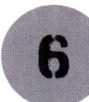

5

Following the curve of your triangle, draw the shoulders. On the left side, add a small lump, but otherwise, draw a smooth line that extends past your sketch. Repeat this on the right side but make the line spiky with blowing fur. Afterward, follow the downward curve of your triangle below the left shoulder, leaving a space between the two lines.

6

Add the arms. Overall, the left arm will be oval; this limb is held high and hovers near the chest. The right arm is longer and more rectangular; this limb helps hold and balance the creature upright. Draw spiky fur on the bottom of the left arm and on the right side of the right arm.

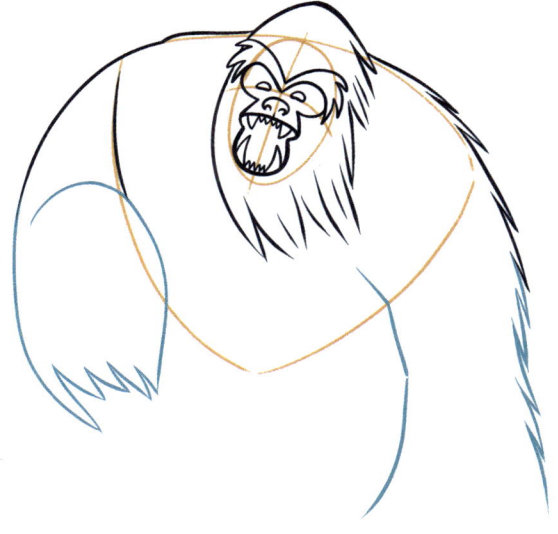

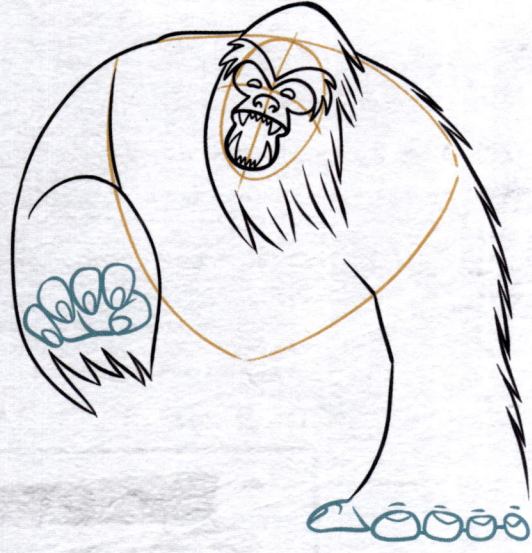

Next, draw the hands. The left hand is curled, whereas the right hand is spread open. Inside the bottom of the left arm's shape, draw four rounded triangles for fingers. On the right, draw a boxy thumb. Afterward, join the pinky and thumb by drawing a palm. For the right hand, draw four rounded squares under the right arm; then, add a long thumb to the left. Add fingernails to each digit, a palm line on the left hand, and detail marks around the fingers of the right hand.

Below and behind the arms, draw the Yeti's legs and feet. First, draw the waist under your sketch. Next, on the left side, draw a curving knee below the arm's fur. Then, under the knee and on the leg's right side, draw spiky fur that connects to the waist. Below the left edge of the fur, draw a foot made of three overlapping clawed toes. Draw the visible portions of the creature's flat sole and round heel between its fur. Under the right side of the waist, draw the right leg; it is mostly obscured by the right arm. Under the armpit, draw an angle to show where the leg is bending at the waist.

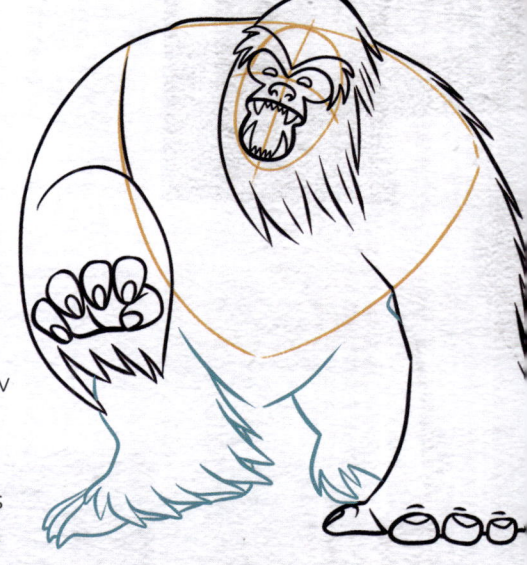

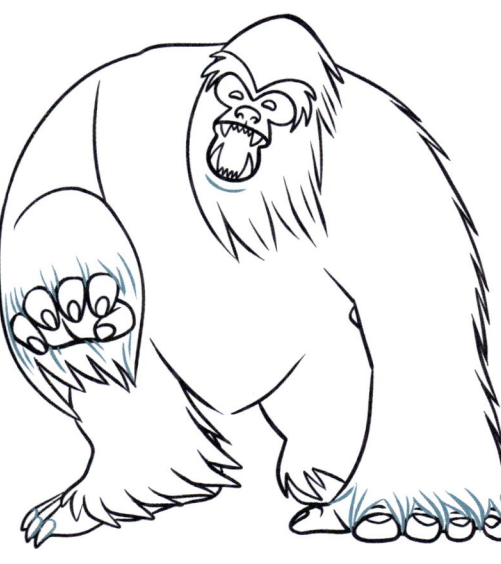

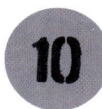

9

Add a few details to the Yeti. Draw the bottom lip and add toenails. Afterward, add gentle curves and spikes around the creature's fingers and palm. This shows that fur hangs between the fingers and falls off the wrist.

10

Erase your sketch lines. Add texture to the body: Draw wavy lines, pointed marks, and dashes at a downward, left-to-right angle to show the direction the wind is blowing.

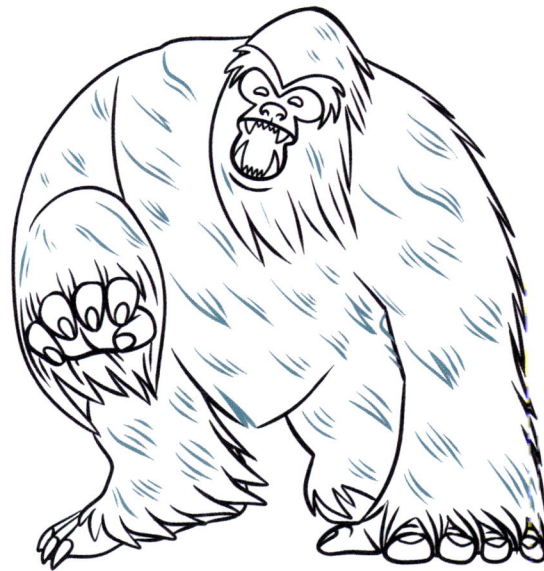

Ahool

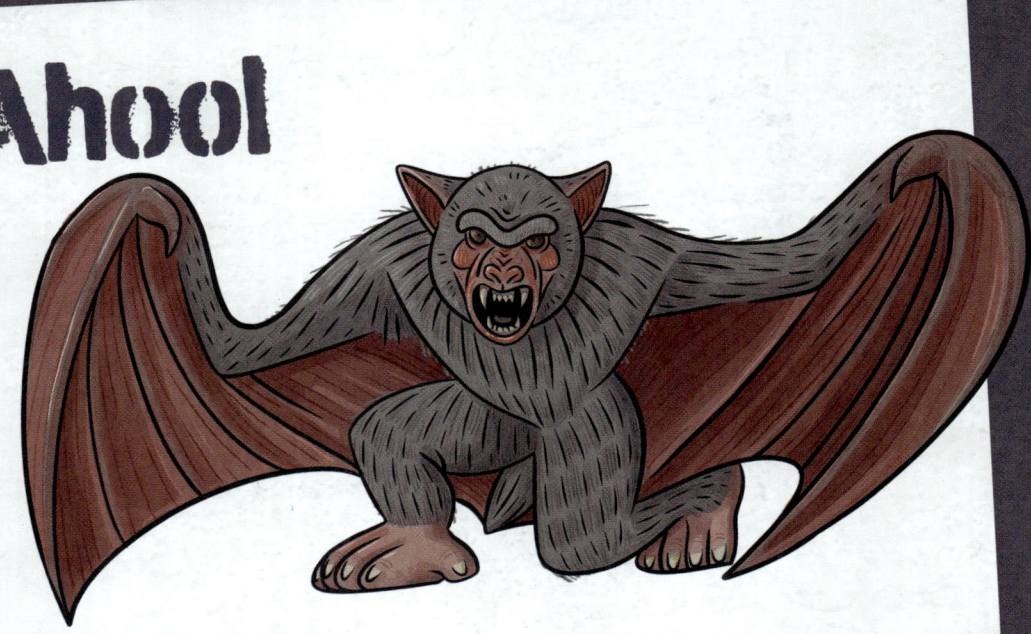

Hiding during the day, a giant, flying creature waits for the sun to set in Java, Indonesia. Only under the cover of darkness does the Ahool hunt. Found throughout the rainforest, it is described as an enormous, red-skinned bat or gorilla with wings that stretch eighteen to twenty-eight feet (6 to 9 m).

Even though it is covered in soft, gray fur, this cryptid is not cute or cuddly. A carnivorous animal that mainly survives on fish, it prefers larger meals. Peering from trees with dark, beady eyes, it may swoop down and capture campers or hikers wandering outside at night.

Its name is based on the sound it makes before attacking: a two-syllable cry of *A – hool*. It has been most frequently encountered around Mount Salak.

1

Sketch a circle. In the middle of the shape, add a vertical guideline and a curved horizontal guideline. Around your circle, sketch a rounded triangle. The circle should not be in the triangle's center but above and to its left.

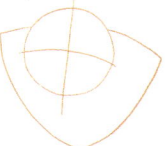

2

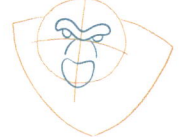

Using your guidelines, draw the Ahool's face, a wormlike shape. Add a unibrow in the center of your guidelines. Below each side, draw an eye. Next, draw the Ahool's snout. Under it, draw the cryptid's open mouth.

3

Draw the Ahool's triangular ears, as well as their insides. Draw the bottom lip. Use your sketch as a guide to draw the outline of the head; these lines should pass through the top and bottom inner sides of each ear, but not connect.

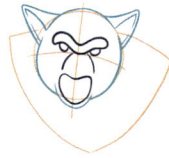

FUN FACT

To the east on Seram Island lives another flying cryptid primate: the Orang Bati. Stories of this creature are much older than the Ahool's, predating the sixteenth century.

Add details to the face. Give the cryptid an angry expression with a scrunched brow and snarling fangs. Then, add a single dot to each eye. Next, draw the outer eye and cheeks. Lastly, add the Ahool's gorilla-like nose.

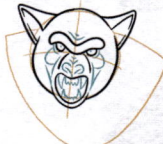

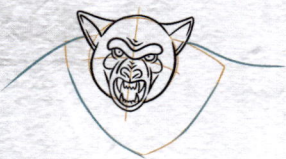

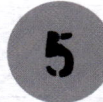

On each side of your triangle sketch, draw the Ahool's shoulders. Use your sketch as a guide to draw the left and right side of its chest. Make sure to leave space below each shoulder and at the bottom of the chest.

Under your sketch, draw the cryptid's legs. One leg is held up, whereas the other rests on the ground. Then draw the Ahool's foot under the left leg. The cryptid has four chunky toes and a short thumb. Between its legs, add a wedge-shaped tail.

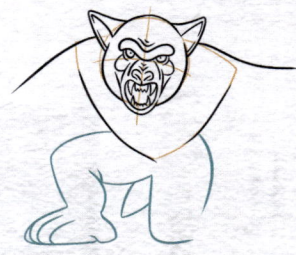

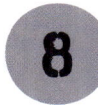

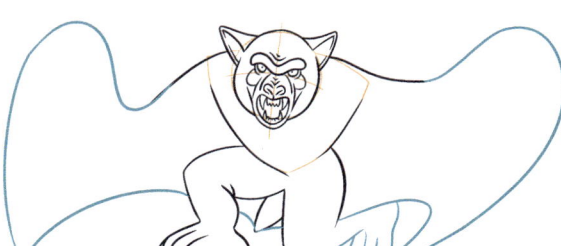

7

Extending from each shoulder, draw the top of the Ahool's wings. They should end aligned to the creature's foot. Then connect the wings to the body and tail; make each wingtip sharp and pointy. Below the right wing, draw the Ahool's other foot; this one is pointed downward.

8

Where each wing bends, draw a clawed thumb facing the Ahool and pointing downward. Below each thumb, draw the arm. Afterward, draw a series of curving lines from the outer side of the wing to the inner side of the wing. Lines on the left wing will overlap as the arm is curled in on itself.

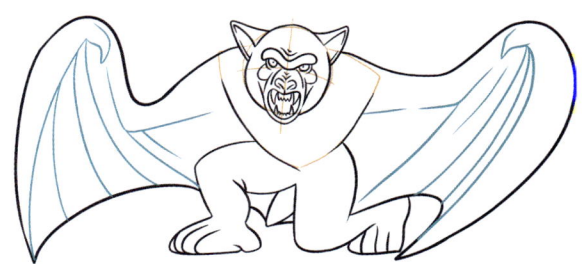

9

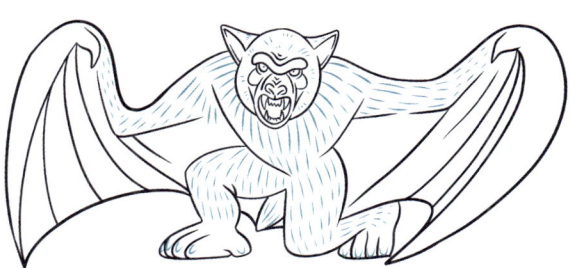

Erase your sketch lines. To finish the Ahool, draw its fur; its fur is longer on its chest and tail and shortest on its face. Be mindful of the direction of your lines. Lastly, add toenails.

SWAMP-LURKING
CRYPTIDS

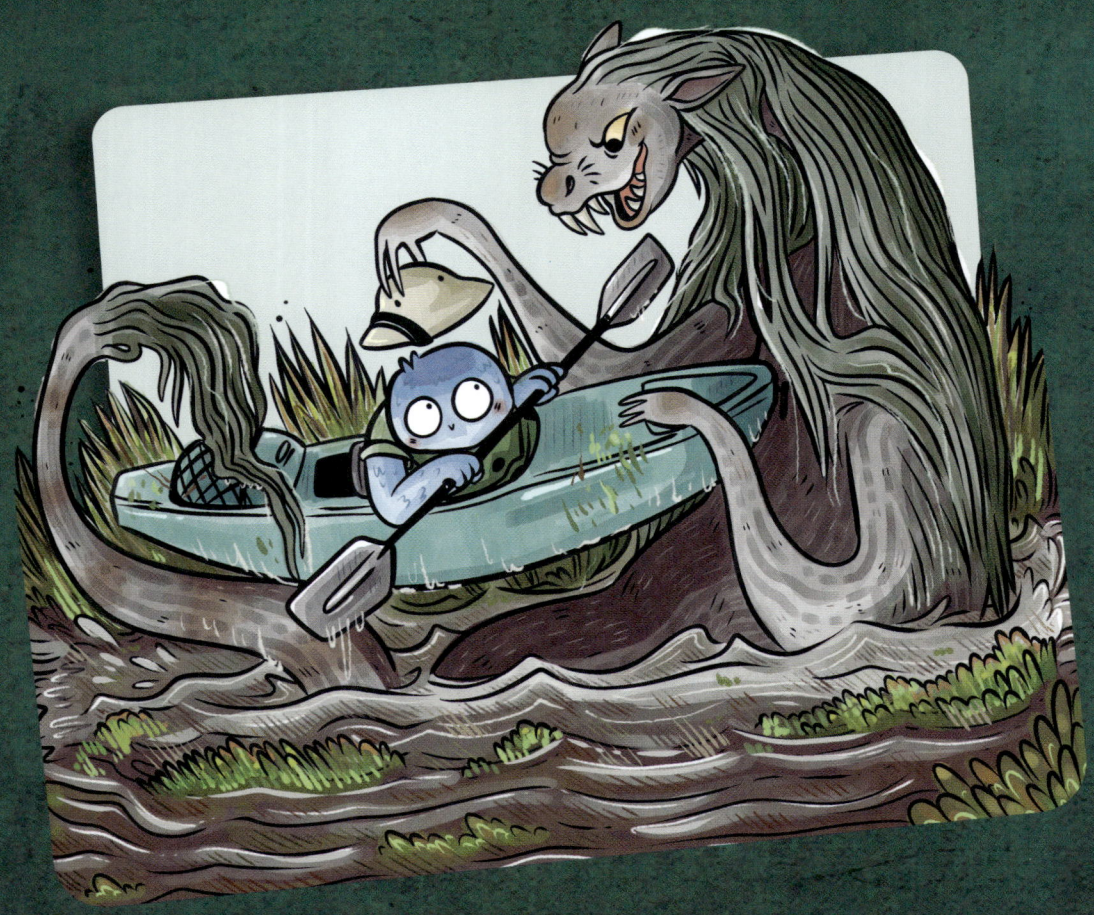

Highly vegetated, deeply muddy, and permanently waterlogged, swamps are habitats that rare—and sometimes dangerous—animals call home. With plenty of hiding places, creatures lurk under dark, scummy water and behind bulky tree trunks, tall ferns, or dense shrubs. Difficult to navigate and bustling with life, the swamp is also perfect for cryptids. From giant, smelly primates to prehistoric reptiles and unusual amphibians, cryptids from the swamp blend into the wetland's murky colors, waiting for their next meal.

Mokèlé-Mbèmbé

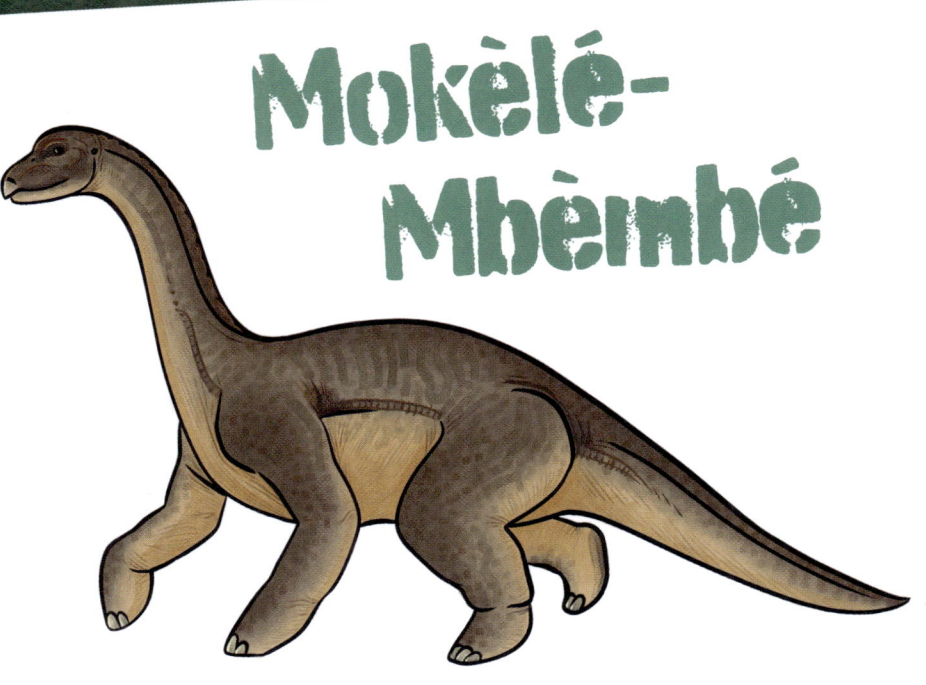

The Mokèlé-Mbèmbé is a four-legged behemoth that wanders the Congo River Basin in Central Africa. The cryptid is said to have smooth skin, a lengthy neck, a powerful tail, and a single tooth or horn on its snout; it can grow as long as thirty-two (10 m) feet and as tall as ten (3 m) feet. There is no consensus on what exactly the Mokèlé-Mbèmbé looks like. While traditional depictions are closer to that of a dinosaur, modern imaginings have transformed it into a sauropod, like the *Diplodocus* genus.

An herbivorous animal, the Mokèlé-Mbèmbé picks leaves from tall trees and any other vegetation it can reach. Though the cryptid eats plants, it is not a peaceful, gentle beast. Stories warn that the Mokèlé-Mbèmbé spends most of its time hiding underwater; if a boat passes by the creature, it will burst from the water, overturn the vessel, and violently bite and lash out at its passengers.

1

Sketch the round bean shape of the creature's body. Then, on the left side, sketch a long, upward curve. To the right side, sketch a smoother, downward sloping line that curves at the end.

2

Use your sketch as a guide to draw a line from the tip of the head to the end of the tail.

3

Draw Mokèlé-Mbèmbé's face. Create a sloped snout that comes to a toothy point and long smile. Afterward, draw the lower jaw below; this line should reach the height of the snout's beginning. Above, add the ear by drawing and coloring in a small circle. Then, in the center of the head, draw a small, circular eye. Add a dot for its nostril.

4

Draw the neck. This line should follow the same curves as the upper neck. Widen the neck's shape the closer it gets to the body.

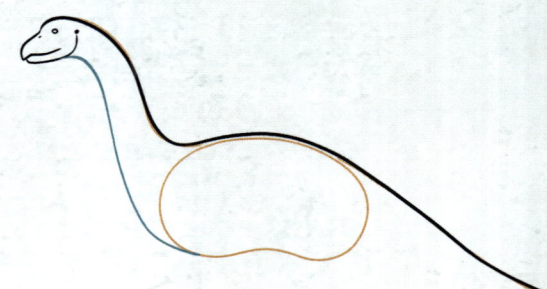

5

Add the cryptid's thick, blocky front legs. Draw the first leg to the left of the neck; this leg is stepping forward. Draw the second leg similarly, but to the right of the neck.

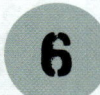

6

Similar to Step 5, draw the back leg; this limb is wider and pointed to the left instead of to the right. Leave a gap between the thigh and tail. Lastly, using your sketch as a guide, draw a line between the front and back legs.

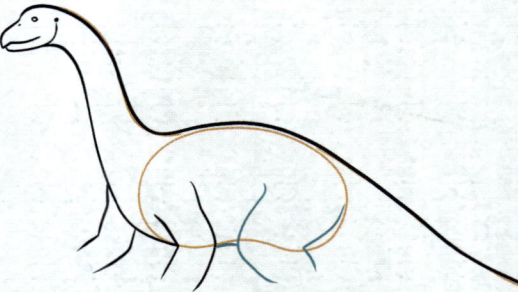

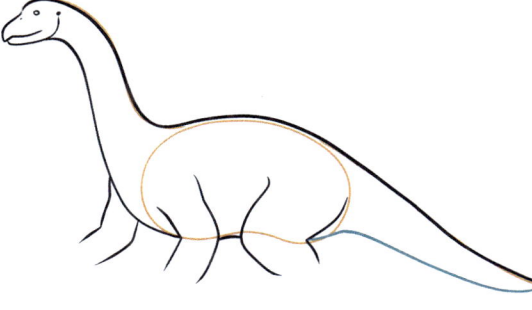

7

As you drew the neck in Step 4, draw the bottom of the tail. Using your sketch as a guide, draw a round hump behind the back leg. Then, draw a downward sloping line that follows the curve of the upper tail. Unlike the neck, the tail will taper toward the end.

8

Draw Mokèlé-Mbèmbé's feet. Start with the back feet, which are round, wedge shapes. Draw the lower leg before adding each foot. Then draw the cryptid's front feet. The leftmost leg's foot is pointed downward; the foot to the right is pressing down on the ground, causing its shape to be flat on the bottom.

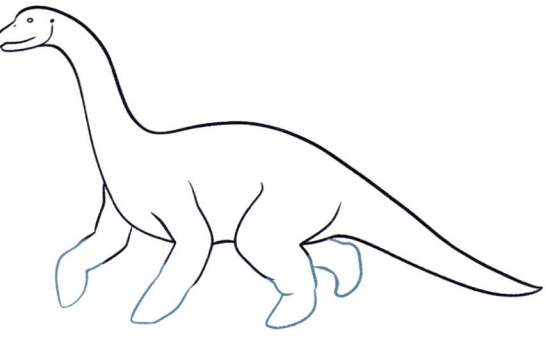

9

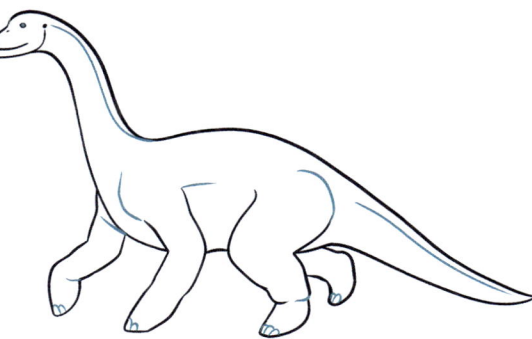

Erase your sketch lines. Next, add details to Mokèlé-Mbèmbé. Draw a curve on its snout and color in its eye. Add a curve along the neck and tail to show they are ridged. Add skin folds around the shoulders and ankles. Lastly, draw two or three toenails on each foot.

Bunyip

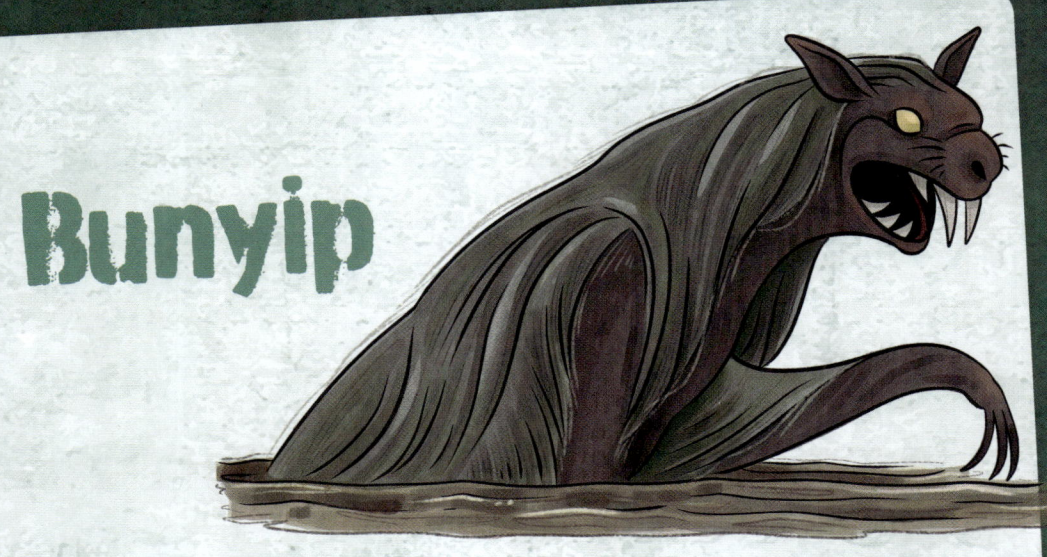

The Bunyip is an animal from Australian Aboriginal folklore. While its appearance and name vary across the country, it's always associated with slow-moving waters and danger. Most sightings can be described in one of three ways: as a strange swimming dog; a giant, hairy seal; or a bizarre long-necked creature with a small head. Stranger and rarer variants exist, as some recount the cryptid's body to be more starfish-like, with limbs as long as its neck. Accounts put the Bunyip anywhere between five and fifteen feet (1.5 and 4 m) long, possessing a long mane of black or brown hair, as well as a horse's tail.

An amphibious, nocturnal creature, this cryptid stays far away from humans. Though it dislikes people, it is said to enjoy eating them. Incredibly quick swimmers, Bunyips spend their day fishing for meals of crayfish and unlucky passersby.

1

Lightly sketch a wavering line; this will be the water's surface. Then sketch a circle above the water. Curving from the top and going behind the head, sketch the Bunyip's back and bring it down to the water.

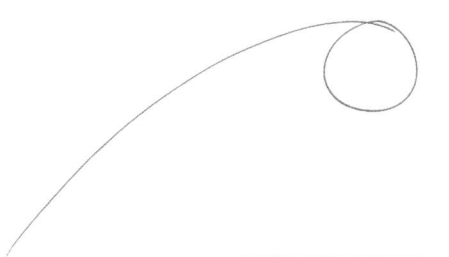

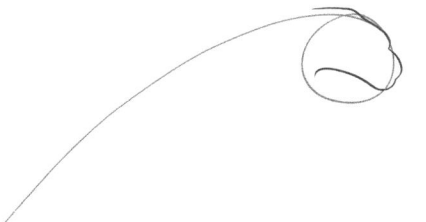

2

Draw the snout. The Bunyip has a thick head of hair, so add a bump at its hairline, as well as one for the ridge of its eyes and where its round nose ends. Bunyips have wide mouths like a dog; draw a long curve almost reaching from side to side of your circle.

3

Add facial features and teeth. This Bunyip combines all three types of sightings; we will give it tusklike teeth, wrinkled skin, large eyes, and whiskers.

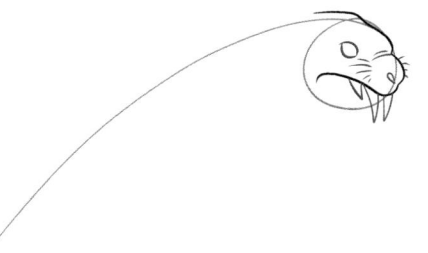

4

Draw the Bunyip's cheek; mouth opened wide, its face will push up against the eye. Draw the lower jaw and lip. The teeth on the bottom are smaller than on the top.

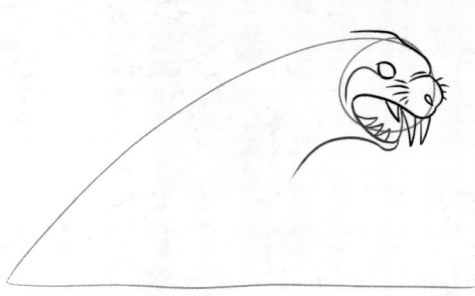

5

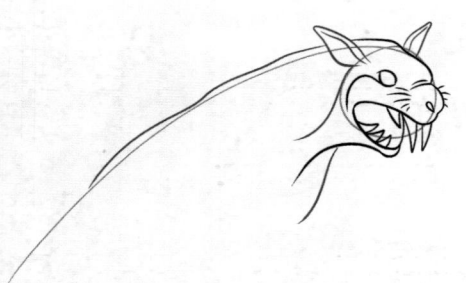

Give the Bunyip long, pointed ears. Following your sketch, draw a wavy line of hair. Then, draw another curve behind the ear, drooping down. Draw another droopy curve behind its neck to show hair flowing off its body.

6

Give the hair texture by drawing long, gently curving lines. Think about how the hair lays on and around the animal, then draw your lines in that direction.

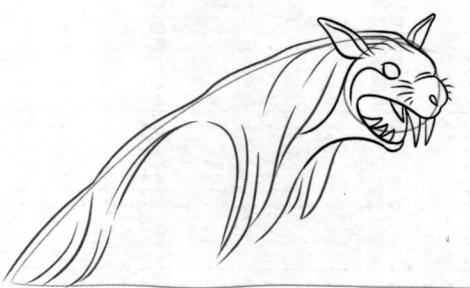

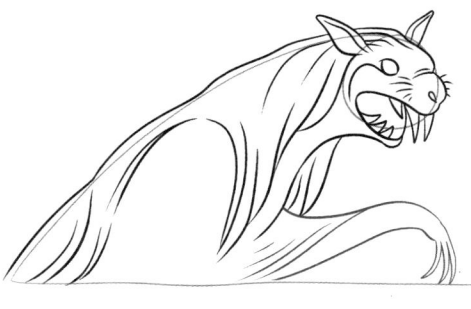

7

Draw the Bunyip's starfish-like arm. On the end, draw a hand with three thin, tapering claws. Add more hair texture on its upper arm.

8

Add curvy lines of texture on the Bunyip's chest and shoulder.

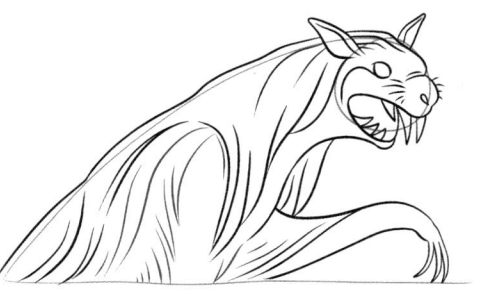

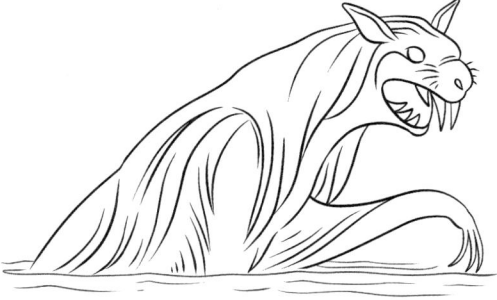

9

Erase your sketch lines and draw water waves around the animal.

FUN FACT

Some people think that the Bunyip may have originated from an extinct marsupial that once lived alongside Australian Aboriginal peoples tens of thousands of years ago.

Loveland Frogman

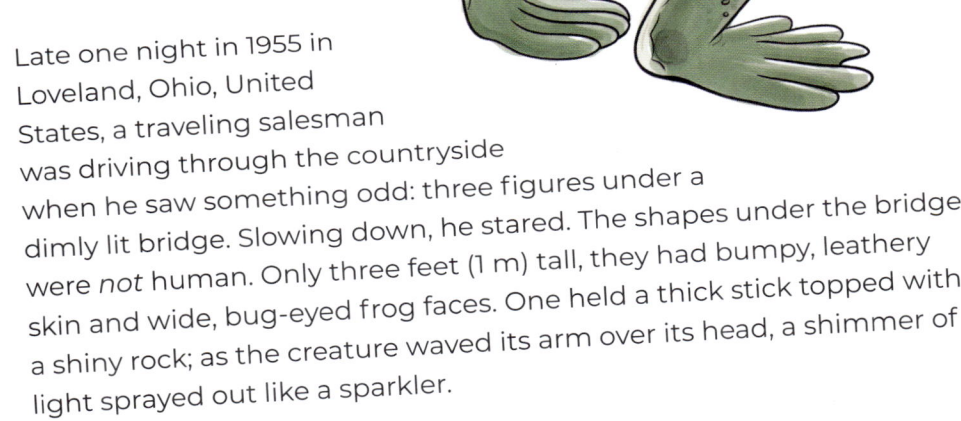

Late one night in 1955 in Loveland, Ohio, United States, a traveling salesman was driving through the countryside when he saw something odd: three figures under a dimly lit bridge. Slowing down, he stared. The shapes under the bridge were *not* human. Only three feet (1 m) tall, they had bumpy, leathery skin and wide, bug-eyed frog faces. One held a thick stick topped with a shiny rock; as the creature waved its arm over its head, a shimmer of light sprayed out like a sparkler.

While the sighting generated a lot of buzz, the "frogmen" were not seen again until 1972. A local policeman was driving alongside the Little Miami River when something jumped in front of his vehicle. Paused atop a guardrail, the creature turned and stared into the car with intelligent eyes before disappearing into the darkness.

1

Sketch a rounded triangle for the Frogman's head. Add a curving arch for its back.

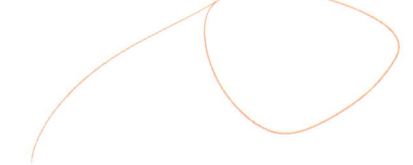

2

Draw a slightly squished circle for the eye; right above it, draw a curve for the eyebrow. A Frogman's back is bumpy, so use your sketch to draw a wavy line.

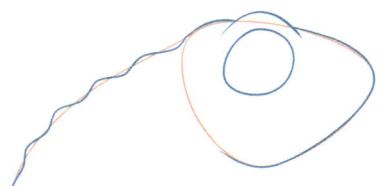

3

Sketch another round shape for the Frogman's body. Then, sketch a few lines for the legs.

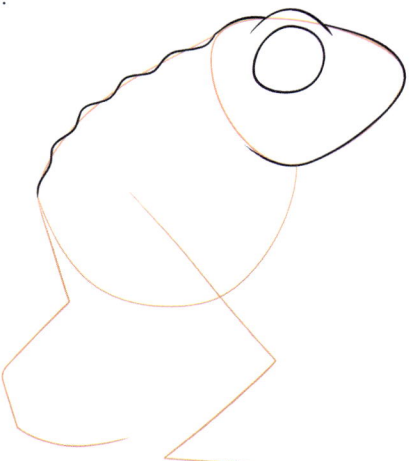

4

Sketch two round shapes for the feet. One foot will be pressing forward to take a step, while the other is spread out for balance.

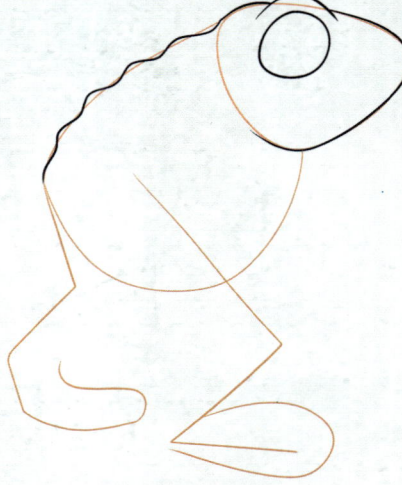

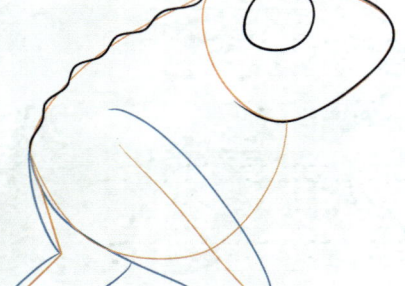

5

Use your sketches as a guide to draw the legs. The top half of the leg will be much wider than the lower half. Then draw the toes; frog toes are like long, rounded rectangles.

6

Like the legs, sketch the arms, adding a circle where the hands would be.

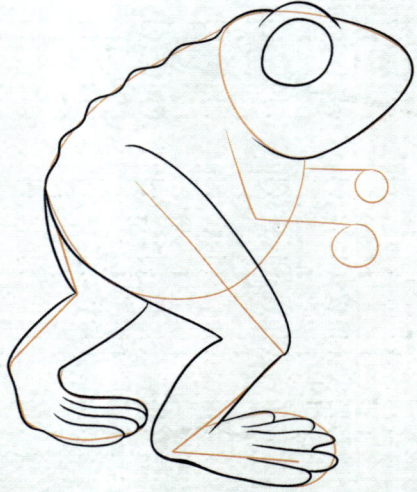

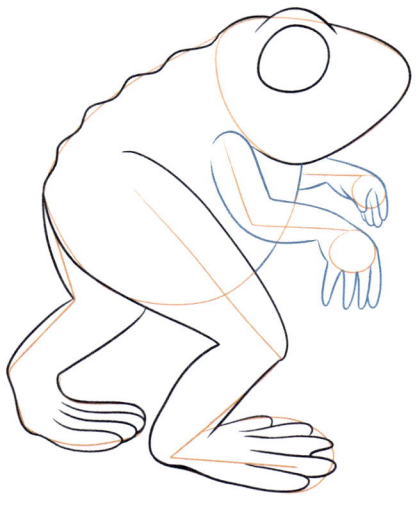

7

Draw arms; the elbow should be nice and round—not sharp! Then draw the hands; a Frogman's fingers are like long, thin, rounded triangles.

8

Erase your sketch lines and give your Frogman a face. The mouth should be one long curve with a semicircle for the cheek. Add a diamond-shaped pupil in the middle of the eye, as well as an oval on the snout.

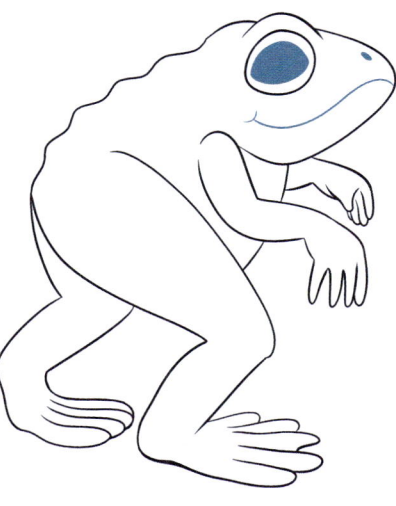

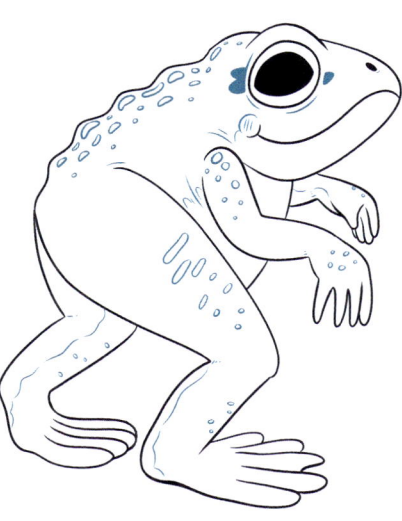

9

Frogs are bumpy animals with colorful patterns! Add wavy lines, curves, circles, and round rectangles to show rough, bumpy skin, warts, and creases; draw a thin, wavering line in the middle of the torso and each leg to show where the frog's back ends and its soft underside begins.

LIZARDMAN OF SCAPE ORE SWAMP

On the outskirts of the Scape Ore Swamp in Browntown, South Carolina, United States, lives the Lizardman. Sludging through mud, hunching in bushes, and peering from under the water, it is a dangerous entity. Green and scaly, the Lizardman is shiny with slime or water; standing seven feet (2 m) tall, it has only three fingers on each hand and menacing, bright-red eyes. Said to chase hikers, attack cars, and steal pets, reports of Lizardman activity occur not only in the surrounding swampland but also in local sewer systems.

First documented in 1987, its most infamous encounter occurred on June 29, 1988. Early that morning, a man saw a creature running toward him while he was parked on the side of the road. Hopping back into his car, the monster followed, leaping onto the car's roof. Speeding ahead, the man sent the creature tumbling off the side, breaking the car's mirror.

1

Sketch a tall oval. Below its center, sketch a horizontal, curving guideline that angles slightly upward. Next, from the top of your oval, sketch a long, curving line to the right.

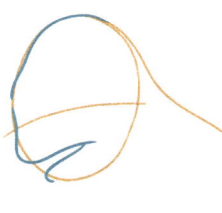

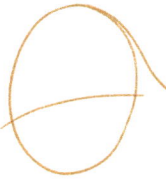

2

Use your sketch as a guide to draw the top of the Lizardman's head. The forehead will dip inward briefly at the bottom. Afterward, draw the creature's snout and mouth. Leave space between this section and the forehead.

3

Add the Lizardman's eyebrows. Below the right eyebrow, draw a sharp eye. The upper lid will curve past the eye and match the curve of the brow. In the center of the eye, draw a curved dash for its snakelike pupil. Add the lower eyelid. Draw two curvy cheek creases. Add a nostril on the tip of the snout and a round, circular ear hole on the right side of the head.

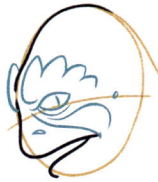

4

Add texture to the Lizardman's lips by drawing a series of overlapping, rounded rectangles. Between the lips, draw tiny, pointed teeth; add as many fangs as you can!

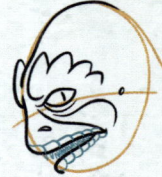

5

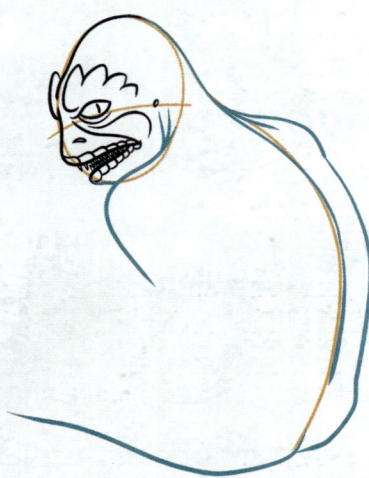

Use your sketch as a guide to draw the Lizardman's neck, back, and shoulders. Add creases around the lower jaw and right shoulder. Copy the curve of the spine and draw the rest of the back under the right shoulder. Then, draw a squarish curve that ends at the base of your sketch. A bit above, and briefly following your sketch, draw a similar curve that extends left and upward diagonally. It should reach past the head.

6

Under the left shoulder, draw the left arm. This limb has a pointed elbow, is bent, and reaches to the left. A muscular cryptid, make the shape thick and bulky. Add a few creases on the top right of the arm.

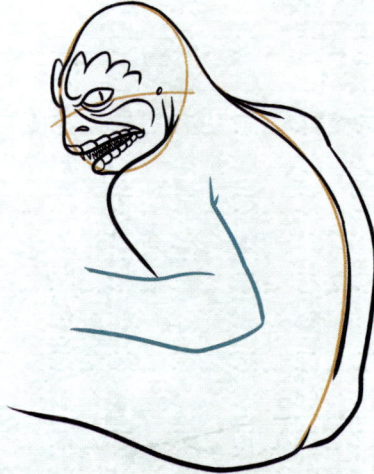

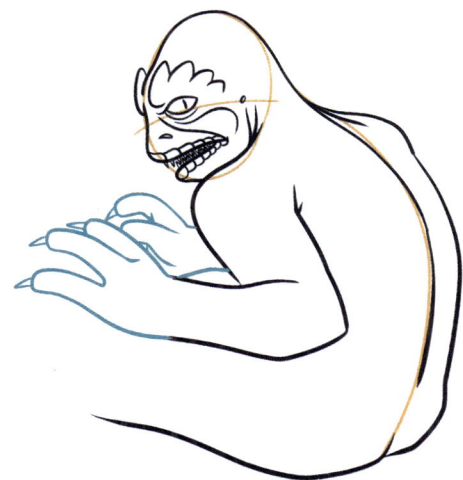

Draw the Lizardman's hands. This cryptid has only three long fingers; each digit is the same size and ends with a small, sharp claw. Much of the right hand is hidden from view. For this hand, draw two long, curving fingers.

Draw the left leg and both feet. Under the left hand, draw the round curve of the knee, which rounds into a second, downward, right-leaning slope. Draw creases for the ankle to the right. Under the leg, draw a dinosaur foot. The left foot is comprised of three identical sloping curves. To its right, draw the bend of the heel and ankle. Under the sketch of the spine, draw a V. Below, add a W. Next, draw and color in three claws on the left foot.

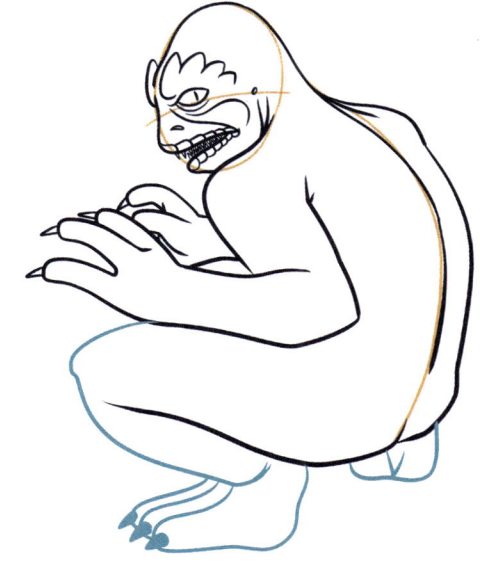

Erase your sketch lines. Lastly, add texture by giving the creature scaly skin. Finally, add sharp spines along the neck and back like an iguana.

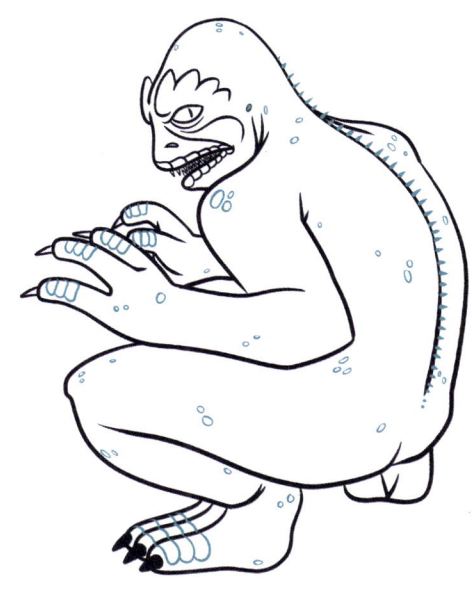

Sasquatch

Sasquatch (or Bigfoot) is a large, hairy creature that has been seen throughout North America. Walking on two oversized feet, they hide behind trees, steal from campsites, and enjoy throwing rocks. According to stories, Sasquatches are as varied as people; they have different fur colors, body types, favorite foods, and personalities. Sasquatches can be benevolent, helping lost children, or malicious, following and terrorizing victims. All, however, are very tall and intelligent.

Sasquatches are the most popular cryptid—and also the most hunted! People search for prints in mud and for clumps of hair on branches, hoping the signs will lead them to one. Cryptozoologists also listen for strange sounds in the woods, like bloodcurdling howls, high-pitched screams, or loud, knocking sounds; in a practice called wood-knocking, some researchers try to draw Sasquatches closer by hitting tree trunks and rocks with large pieces of wood.

1

Sketch a circle; inside, sketch a rounded horizontal and vertical guideline through its center. Around the circle, sketch a large rectangle.

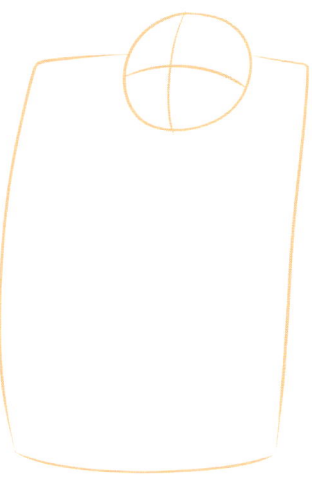

2

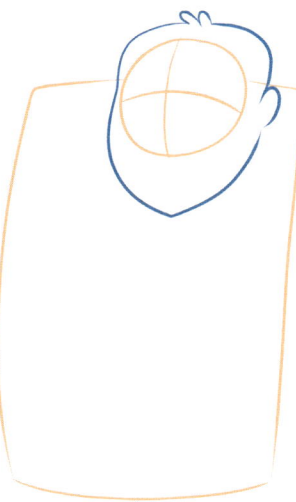

Next, draw the head. Use the horizontal guideline to place the ear; the bottom of the ear should line up with this curve. Sasquatches are furry, fluffy creatures, so their fur will extend past our circle. Give them a pointed beard and a bit of unruly fur on top.

3

Draw two sets of curving lines. These will be the Sasquatch's shoulders and arms.

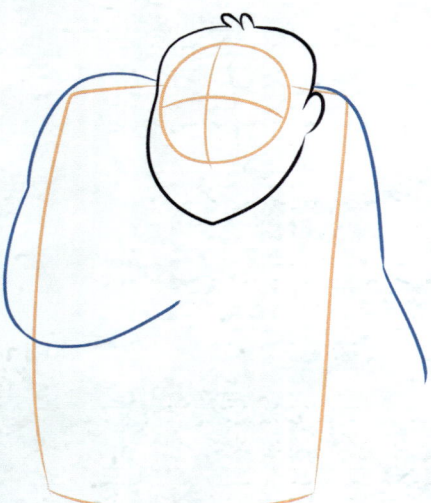

FUN FACT

Sasquatch comes from the word *sasq'ets*, which means "hairy man" in Halq'eméylem, an Indigenous dialect spoken by the Sts'ailes people in what is now known as British Columbia, Canada.

4

Draw the rest of the left arm, then add hands. This cryptid is broad and powerful; giving them thick, bubbly arms and fingers will help them look big and strong.

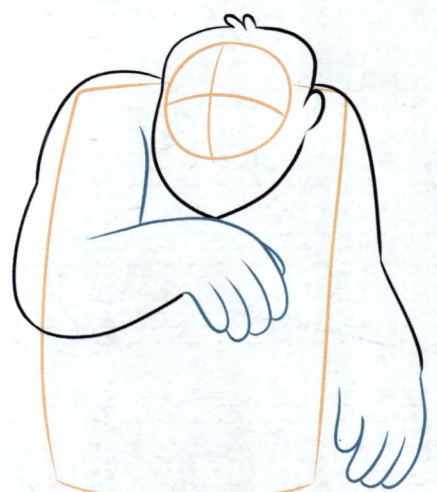

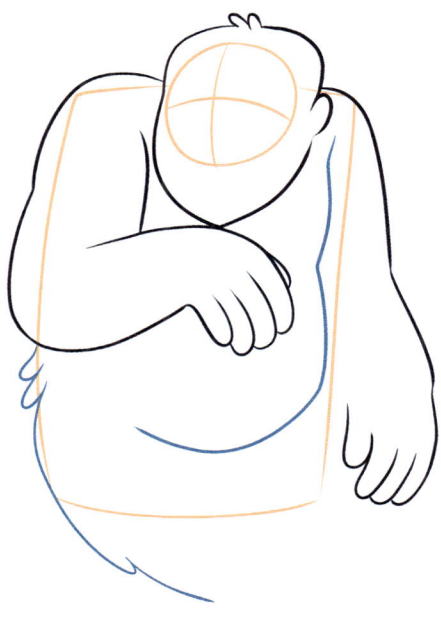

Draw the chest and stomach. Most Sasquatches are said to have large, round bellies. Next, follow the rectangle and draw a few pieces of fluffy hair under the elbow. Connected to the fluff, continue with a rounded curve that shifts to the right; part of the leg, this line will fall below and past your rectangular sketch.

Add hair lines to the hand. Sasquatches have no fur on their hands, feet, or faces; a squiggly line will show where their coat of fur begins!

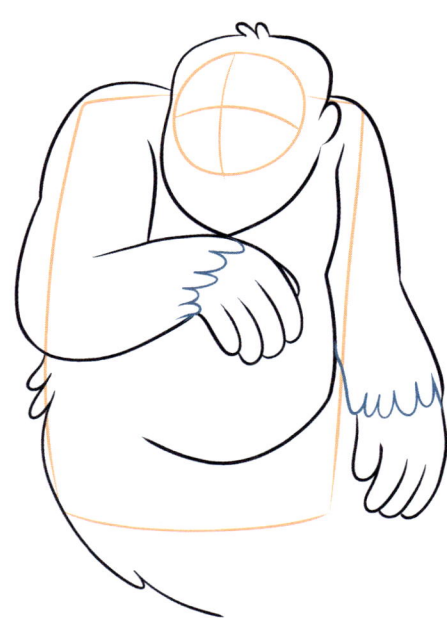

7

Draw the rest of the legs. One is moving in front of the other, so it will be larger. Add the same fur lines used in the last step to show not only where the fur ends at the feet, but also where the kneecap is.

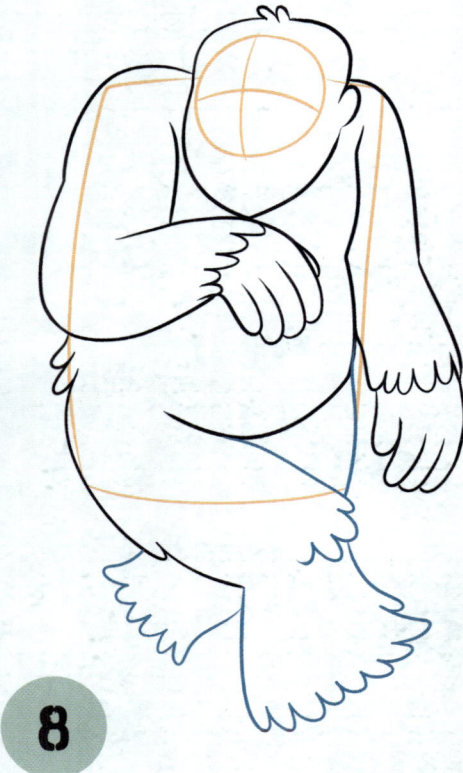

8

Draw the feet. You can lightly sketch a rectangle for each to use as a guide. While the left foot's toes are like the hands we drew, the right foot's toes are a series of overlapping balls.

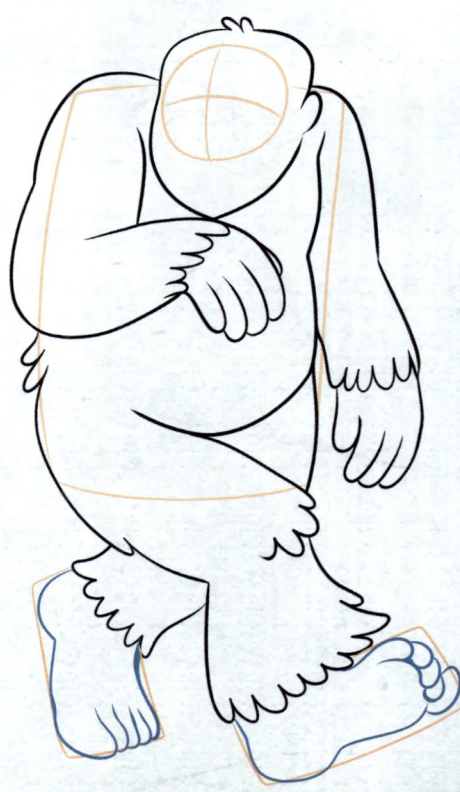

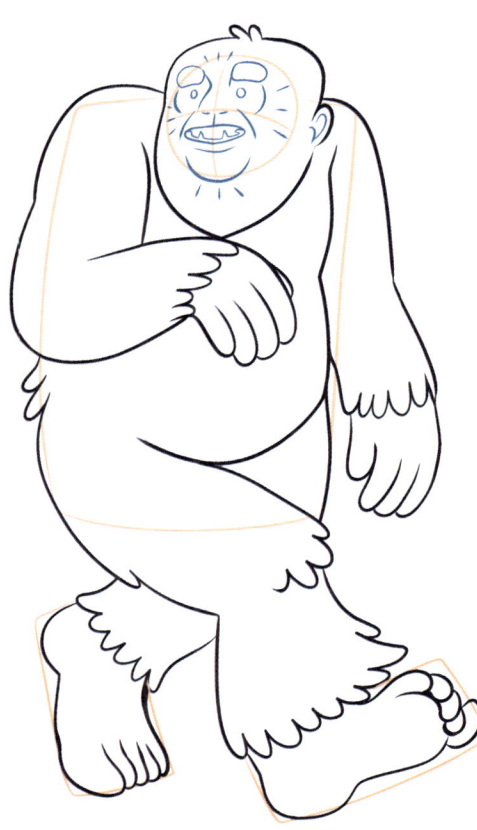

9

Use the guidelines to draw Sasquatch's face: two chunky eyebrows, small circular eyes, an apish nose, a wide mouth, and a round chin. Add a few lines around the face for fur and draw the inner ear.

10

Erase your sketch lines. Add small lines and squiggles to make Sasquatch look furry and to show where their body bends. Add a few details to the hands and feet by drawing small curves to make fingernails and toenails; draw a few stretch lines on the bottom of the foot, too. Lastly, include a small curly line on the belly to make a belly button.

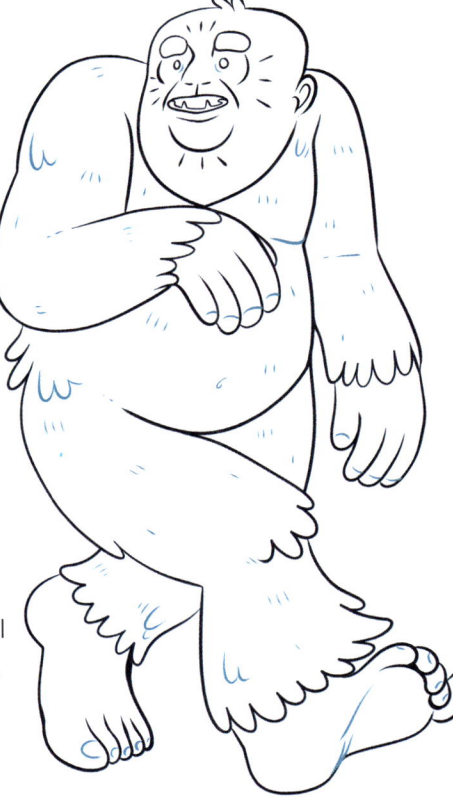

WATER-DWELLING
CRYPTIDS

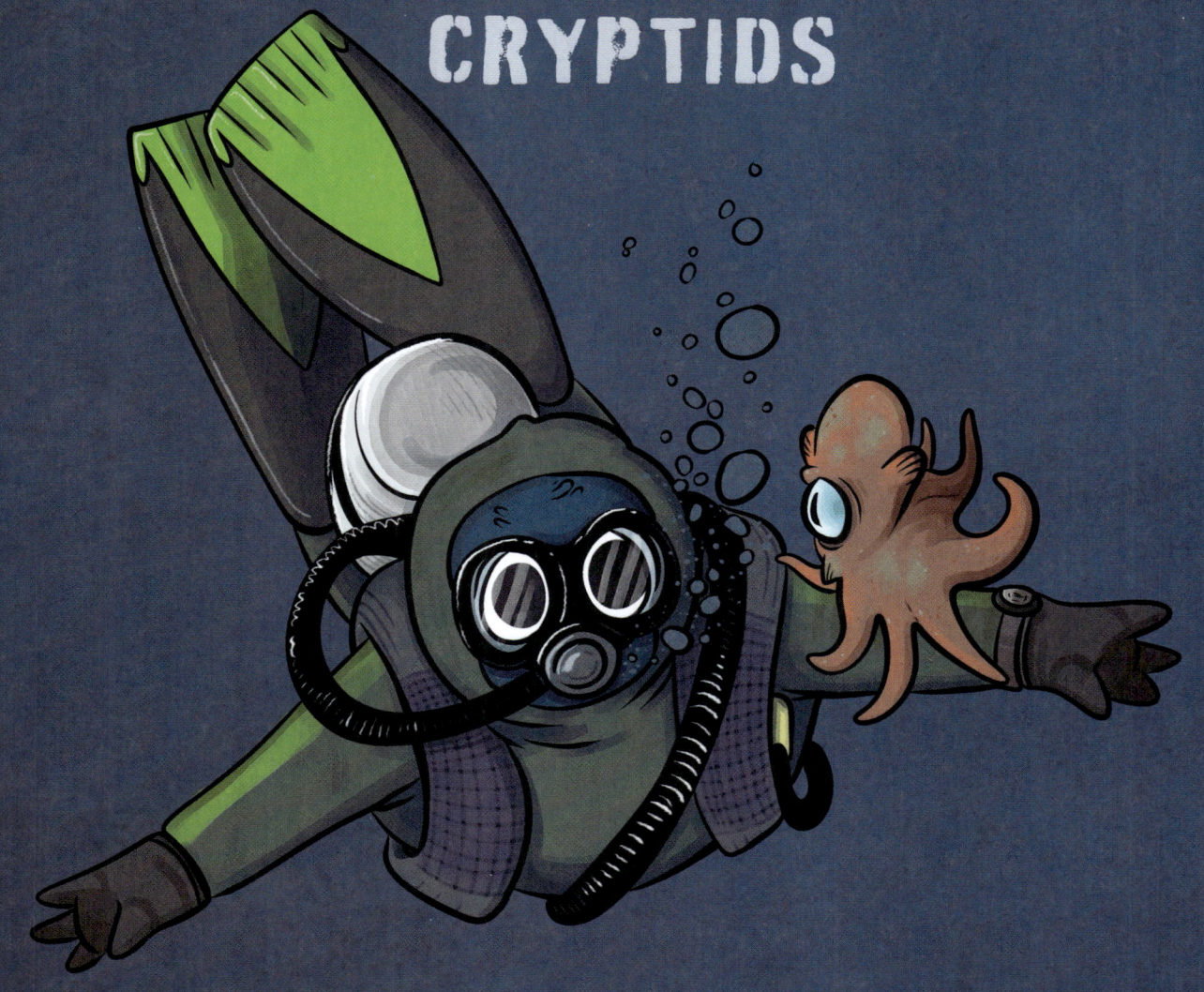

Bodies of water are mysterious. Their depths can be obscured by clouds of sediment or be too rough or inaccessible to explore without specialized equipment. Far from reach, monsters lurk on lake bottoms, inside underwater caves, remote rivers, and the deep sea. Some have violently exploded from the water or slipped from a fishing net; others have only been briefly spotted in dark hiding spots or on the water's surface, diving out of sight as soon as they're seen.

Fur-Bearing Trout

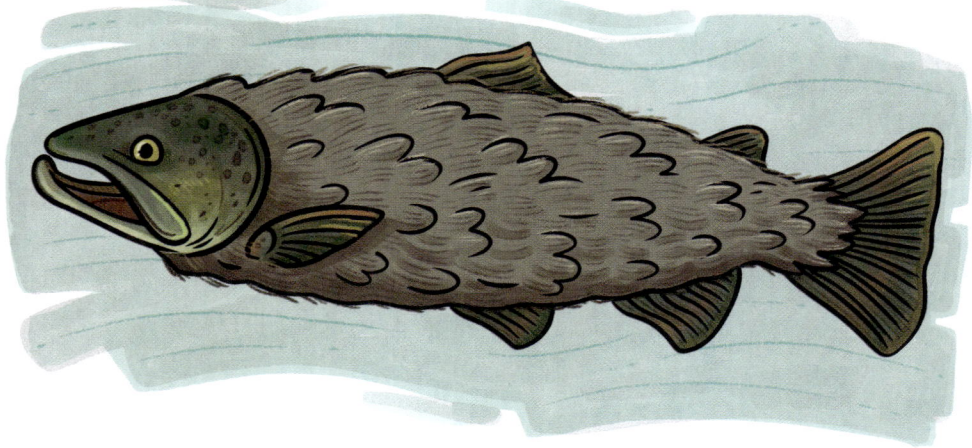

The Fur-Bearing Trout is an American hoax. According to stories, sightings of the animal date back to the 1600s, when Europeans were exploring North America. Seeing fish with furry bodies, these explorers wrote home to their families, recounting vivid descriptions of the odd fish. It was explained that the lakes and rivers of North America grew so cold in the winter that the trout evolved a seasonal coat of fur to stay warm and survive. Some storytellers had an alternative explanation for the trout's fur. In their stories, several jugs of hair tonic spilled into the river, forever changing their—and their offspring's—bodies.

Numerous taxidermy specimens were created in the nineteenth and twentieth centuries in an attempt to provide proof of the animal. Some were preserved and are displayed in museums today.

1

Sketch an almond shape for the fish's body. On the left side, sketch a circle that fits almost perfectly inside and does not cross over the outer shape's lines.

2

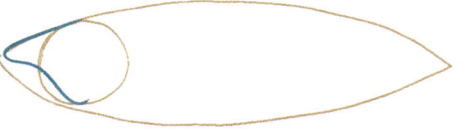

Following the lines of your sketch, draw the top of the head. Before you reach the sketch's left point, draw a tight curve that winds diagonally to the right, looping up at the end. This is the beginning of the fish's mouth.

3

Next, add the bottom jaw. Under the lower right-hand side of the lip, draw an upward-sloping line. It will *not* follow the curve of your sketch. Once the line is under the point of your sketch, draw an arch; this line will continue horizontally and connect to the upper lip. Inside, draw a triangle that copies the curves of the jaw lines. The triangle's bottom line will extend past the upper line, almost connecting to the bump on the lower lip.

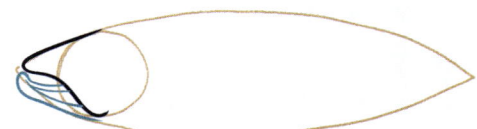

4

Add details to the Fur-Bearing Trout's face. First, draw a flap of skin above the lip. Above the flap, draw a round eye with a flat bottom and its pupil. Next, draw two small curves to the right of the mouth. Following your sketch, draw a semicircle from below the mouth to the top of the head. Lastly, draw a curve inside the center of your last line, copying its shape.

5

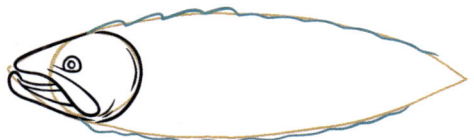

Use your sketch as a guide to draw a wavy line on the top and bottom of your fish's body. These lines should end before getting too close to the sketch's right point. The top line should also be longer than your bottom line. This wave will create a furry hide for the fish.

6

Add fins to the right side of the fish. The top left fin is the only one with a sharp angle—the others are rounded and smooth.

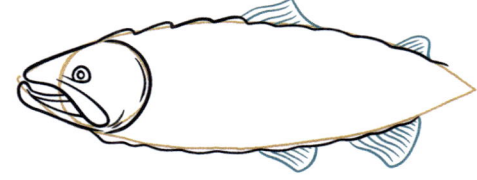

At the far right of your sketch, draw the tail. Start by drawing the fish's furry end with a wavy line loosely following your sketch's shape. Afterward, connect a fin to it. Overall, it will have a triangular shape. Like in Step 6, add wavy interior lines. These will work a bit differently, though. Instead of repeating the same line, those at the top will flare up and straighten as they reach the tail's center. From the center downward, the lines will flare more and more downward.

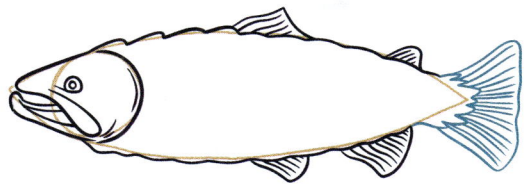

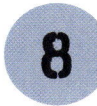

To the right of the head, add the last fin. Unlike the other fins you have drawn, this one is like a tilted teardrop. Within its left, rounded edge, draw a small curve. From this point, curve the interior fin lines outward.

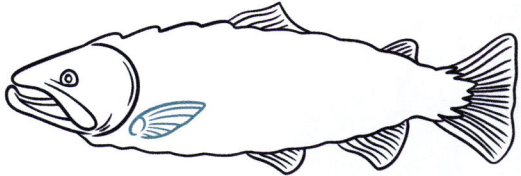

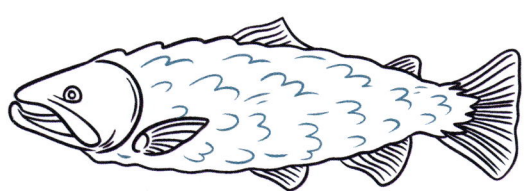

Erase your sketch lines. To finish the drawing, add horizontal, wavy arches, Ws, and lines to give the fish a furry texture. Make sure to only add texture to the furry part of the fish, leaving the head and fins bare.

Loch Ness Monster

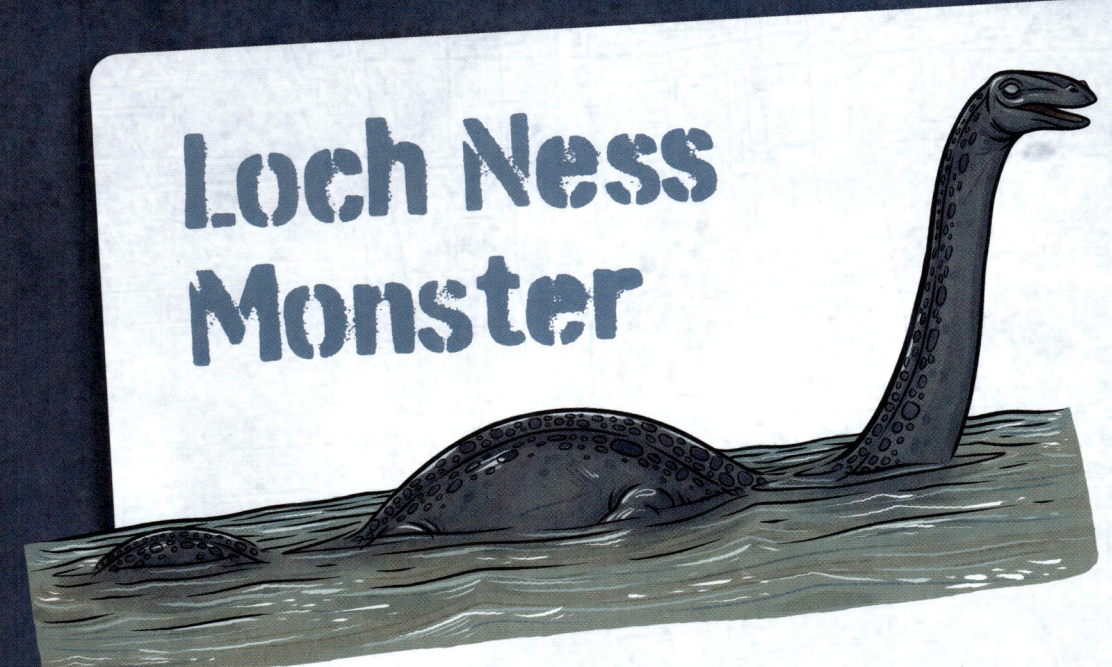

One of the world's most famous cryptids, the Loch Ness Monster is a long-necked creature said to live in Loch Ness in the Scottish Highlands. Nicknamed Nessie, it is usually described as a large, humpbacked cryptid that slithers over the water. Most artists depict Nessie as a plesiosaur—an extinct group of marine reptiles from the Triassic Period.

The most famous Nessie sighting occurred in July 1933. A couple near the lake saw a dragon-like, prehistoric-looking animal cross the road. It was four feet (1 m) tall and twenty-five feet (8 m) long, with a narrow, wavy neck and no discernible limbs. It disappeared into the water quickly. By August, newspapers picked up the story, and the lake bustled with onlookers hoping to catch a glimpse of the creature.

1

Sketch a horizontal line. This will be the surface of the lake.

2

Sketch the Loch Ness Monster's body with two arches and a curve. The beginning of each line and the end of each arch should be below the water line. Each line should also begin and end at roughly the same height. The left line is the cryptid's tail, barely breaching the surface. The middle line is the monster's back. The right line is its tall neck reaching out of the water.

3

Following your sketch, draw the neck, head, and snout. Where the head begins to curve, add a small bump on top of the creature's head.

TIP

The Loch Ness Monster is great to practice drawing different poses with! Sketch it swimming underwater, chasing a fish, or sunning itself with loose, serpentine lines and flapping fins.

Under the head, draw a long, curvy line for the mouth. Under the curve of the mouth, draw a downward slanted line to the right. Next, draw a series of curves at the tip of your last line. Lastly, draw a horizontal teardrop near the tip of the snout.

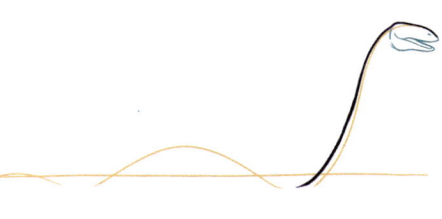

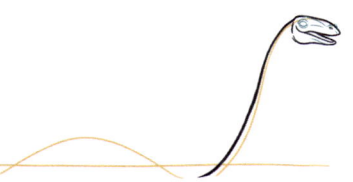

To finish the head, we need to add a few more details. First, color in the cryptid's nostril and draw an arch above it. Then, draw another arch to the right, on top of the snout. Afterward, draw a curve below the nostril to the lip. Extending left from the nose, draw a sloped line that reaches the top of the head. Under it, draw a round curve. Below it, draw the Loch Ness Monster's eye and draw another curve under it. Draw a round curve under the bottom of the mouth to make a lip.

Follow the curve of your previous line and draw the right side of the cryptid's neck. Duplicate the line on the left. Leave a gap in this line near the head.

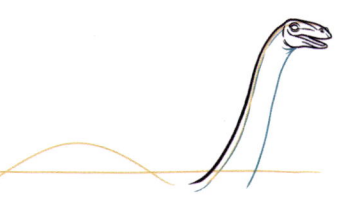

At the base of the neck, draw water lines. Then, draw the monster's back. Like the neck, copy the line on the inside, leaving a few spaces to break it into pieces. Draw a series of round curves to form the animal's arms on the left and right sides of the body. For the left side, you'll only need to draw two left-to-right downward curves. The right side is a bit more complicated. Start with three curves on the right side, drawn like the left arm. These curves shrink in size from left to right. To the left of them, draw a larger curve. Above and touching its left side, draw another left curve. Lastly, in the center of the arm's shape, draw a final right curve. Like at the base of the neck, draw more water lines, swirls, and waves.

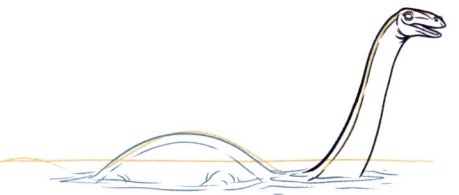

Drawing the tail is very similar to the back. Draw the curve of the cryptid's tail using your sketch as a guide. Copy the line below, leaving gaps in places. Next, draw water lines, swirls, and waves. They will encircle the entire section and pass through some parts of the tail.

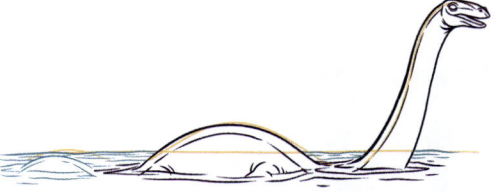

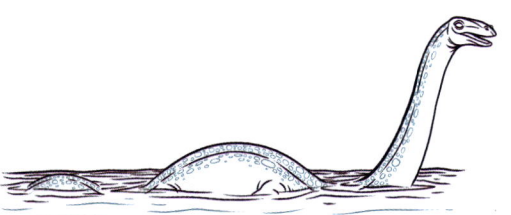

Erase your sketch lines and add decorations to the Loch Ness Monster's spine and upper back and neck. To finish the drawing, add a few gentle waves and lines in front of the cryptid to add more depth.

Lusca

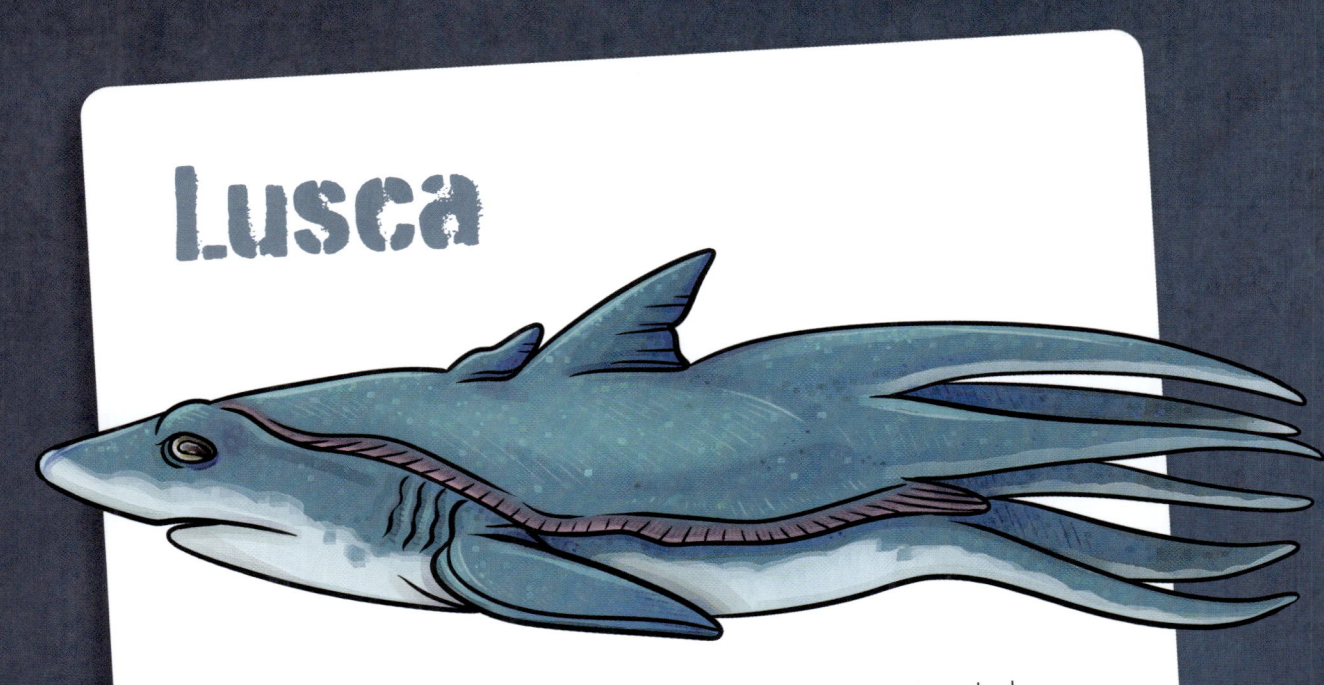

Half shark, half cephalopod, the Lusca is a one or three-headed monstrous cryptid from the Caribbean. It has been described as a cross between a giant cuttlefish, octopus, and tiger shark. According to legend, it is one of the largest sea creatures, growing over seventy-five feet (23 m) long and up to two hundred feet (61 m) long.

The Lusca lives in the Bahamas—more specifically in Andros Island's blue holes. These blue holes are deep cave systems and sinkholes with circular entrances and tall walls. Andros has 178 blue holes, of which 50 lead to the ocean. The Lusca is said to lurk in all of them. Crawling through underwater tunnels and eating what it comes across, the Lusca is a carnivorous creature that can survive in deep or shallow water. Able to flatten its body and stretch its tentacles, the Lusca can also camouflage itself or change color.

1

Sketch a rounded angle pointed to the left.

2

Near the left edge of your sketch, draw an oval with an overhanging curve on its top left. Above it, add a round eyebrow that passes slightly over your sketch.

3

Draw the top of the cryptid's head. On the left, draw the snout; to the right, follow your sketch and draw a line. Then, draw the rest of the shark's nose, extending the curve and curling a little more inside your sketch. Then, add a downward frown to the right.

TIP

For a challenge, try making your Lusca more monstrous by drawing it with three heads. The back head could curve up or down behind the original drawing; another, larger, head could overlap and face the viewer.

4

Add a tight curve under the mouth. It rounds outside your sketch and extends as far right as the top line you drew. Then, on top of the back, draw two shark fins. The one on the left is a third smaller than the fin on the right. The left fin has a bump on the left, and the fin on the right has a sharp notch on its right. Both are rounded, triangular shapes.

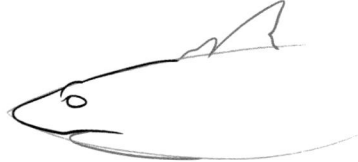

5

Draw a long fin below the fins and on the Lusca's belly. It is a rounded, triangular shape and extends slightly past your fins on the right. Leave a gap in the top left.

6

Next, on the top and bottom of the shark, draw a long curve. The top is a round line, whereas the bottom is wavy. This will become the Lusca's tentacles.

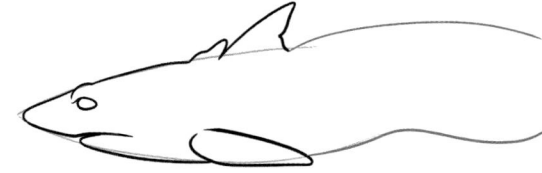

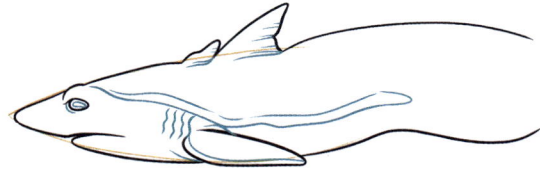

7

Let's add a few details, like those to the fins and on the body. Draw four wavy gills to the left of the flipper. Draw a curve above and below the flipper. Lastly, add a curve to the lower left of the eye and draw a pointed, horizontal pupil inside it.

8

Draw the first layer of tentacles. Two are above the Lusca's horizontal flap of skin and one below.

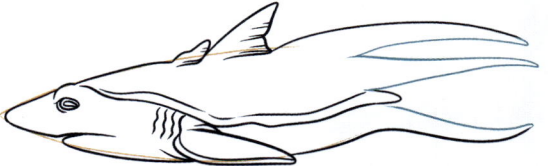

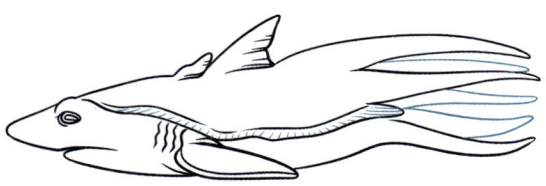

9

Erase your sketch lines, then add the last three tentacles. Of these new tentacles, the top should be wavy, and the bottom should curve upward. To finish, add texture to the Lusca's horizontal fin. Draw slanted lines that point toward the center of the cryptid's body.

Kraken

In the Norwegian Sea swims a colossal creature called the Kraken. One of the oldest cryptids still believed in today, the Kraken of modern times differs from its pre-eighteenth-century versions. Once described as a giant, many-armed or horned fish, later sightings changed its appearance to resemble a whale, crab, or starfish.

While its physique evolved over time, its activities have remained consistent. The Kraken is said to rest with some of its body poking from the water; these exposed parts resemble small islands covered in seaweed. Wherever a Kraken rests, droves of fish can be found. The catch can be so bountiful that anglers have risked their lives for the haul. But fishing on a Kraken poses many dangers. The creature could suddenly descend into the water, creating a deadly whirlpool, or it could snap its arms up and around ships, breaking them in half.

1

Sketch an upside-down, slanted teardrop. Passing through its center, draw a long, diagonal guideline.

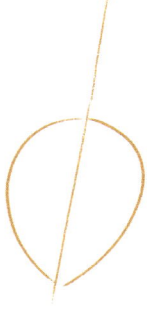

2

Use your sketch as a guide to draw the Kraken's eyebrows. Next, draw the top of the animal's sharp beak between the brows; leave a gap on the top left and right sides. Above the beak, add a few texture lines where the skin furls. These lines should almost touch each side of the brow.

3

Draw the top of the head. Stemming from each brow, draw a round, outward arch that curves back toward the head at its end. Draw a tall arch that connects both head flaps, making its tallest point where your guideline passes through. Lastly, draw two curves above the eyebrows on each side, using your sketch as a guide.

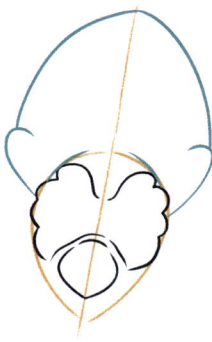

TIP

The Kraken's tentacles can be as long and curly or as straight and short as you like. Tentacles do not require precision, so if they do not turn out exactly like the example or if you want to try something different, that is okay!

4

On each head flap, draw an inner curve. Then, add the Kraken's eyes, including its pupils. Add a curve on the top and bottom outer edges for its eyelids.

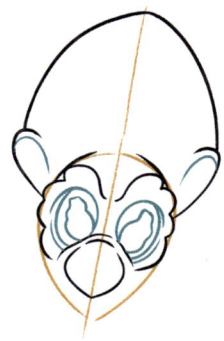

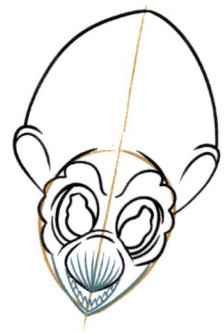

5

On the beak, draw several curved lines that meet at its bottom point. Under the beak, draw the Kraken's open mouth and a series of triangular fangs. Draw the bottom of the Kraken's head.

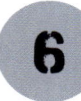

6

The following steps will show you how to add several layers of tentacles. To the right of the head, draw a thick, curling tentacle. To its left, draw a second, more horizontal arm. Add a tiny curve on the top of the head to show that the tentacle is folded. To the left of the head, draw a third tentacle. This arm twists in a spiral. Consider which parts overlap and are visible when drawing this tentacle.

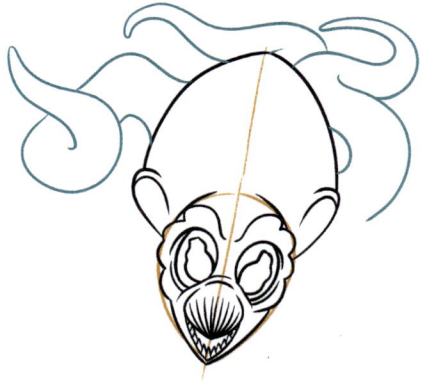

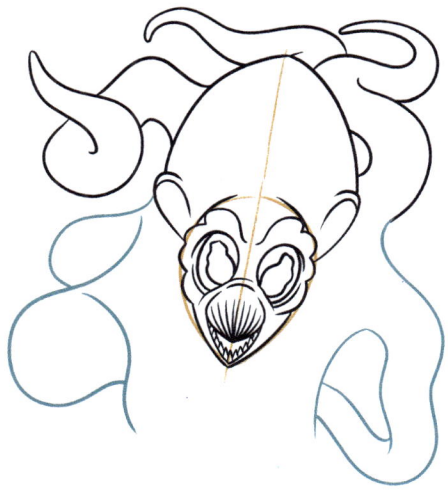

Next, draw curling lines to create parts of the fourth and fifth tentacles. Then, draw a wavy line to the right of the Kraken that connects to the first tentacle. To its left, draw a wavy arch.

Under Step 7's lines, draw a twisting tentacle. Then, add the last tentacle in the lower right side of the drawing. Once this leg is complete, draw the unfinished portions of the other tentacles.

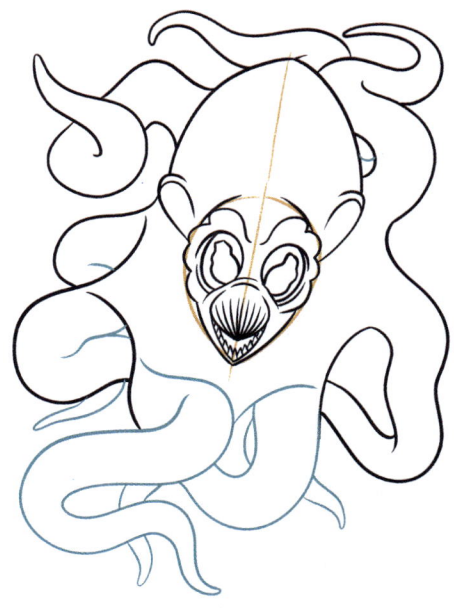

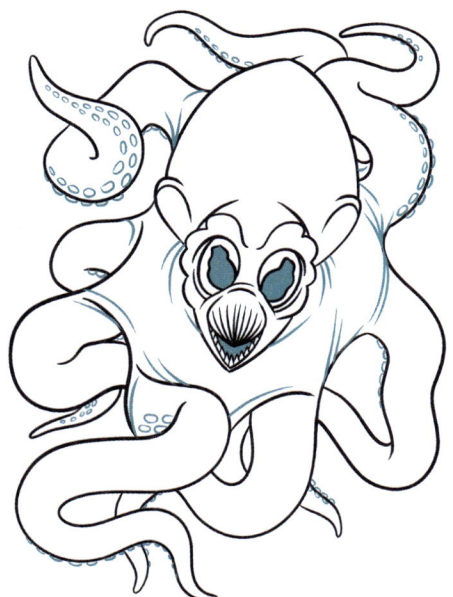

Erase your sketch lines. Then, add details. First, color in the pupils and mouth. Next, draw several curving lines around the head, torso, and base of the legs to show where skin stretches and bunches. To finish, give each tentacle suction cups. Each suction cup is a small oval and appears in rows of two. The cups twist and curl with the creature's arms and grow smaller toward the end of the limb.

Uktena

The Uktena (or Horned Serpent), is a creature from Indigenous mythology predominantly associated with North America in the Great Lakes and Southeastern Woodland peoples. Depicted on rock art, pottery, and elsewhere in archaeological sites, the Uktena varies among cultures. In Cherokee tradition, the Uktena is described as thick as a tree, with glowing scales and a diamond-like crest on its forehead. In Muscogee (Creek) stories, the creature lives underwater; it exposes crystal-like scales, sprawling horns, and a gemstone on its forehead when it emerges. Other cultures separate the serpent into categories based on the color of their horns: red, blue, yellow, and white. Some stories also recount the Uktena as having a pair of feathery wings.

Most cultures, however, link the serpent with the weather and water. The Uktena differs not only physiologically but also psychologically. Stories depict the creature as animalistic, intelligent, and malicious—or extremely deadly and predatory.

1

Sketch the Uktena coming out of the water. First, sketch a horizontal line. Above the water line and on the left, sketch a triangle. On its upper-rightmost point, sketch the tightly curving line of the serpent's body; the line should extend below the water line.

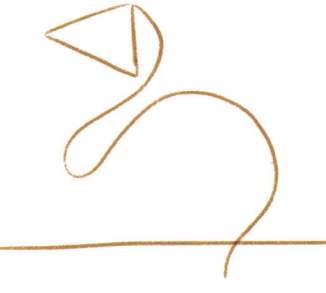

2

Draw the Uktena's gemstone: an almond shape on the top and center of your triangle. Below it, draw the eyebrow, which nearly touches the gem. Under it, draw the eye. Inside, add a serpentine pupil; make sure to curve it to give the eye depth.

3

Draw the Uktena's snout with a line that curves from the gemstone, around the left point of the triangle and rounds into a wide smile. Under the tip of the snout, include a small W.

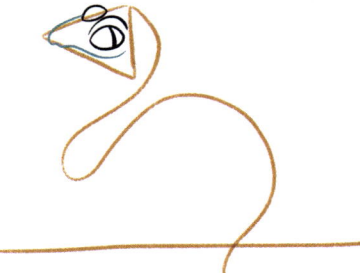

4

From the snake's mouth, draw a long, forked tongue. Below the mouth, draw the bottom jaw; this line curves past the snake's smile and the sketched triangle. Lastly, add a nostril above the mouth.

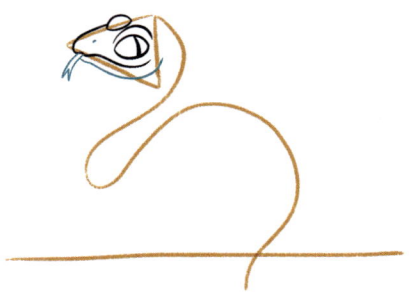

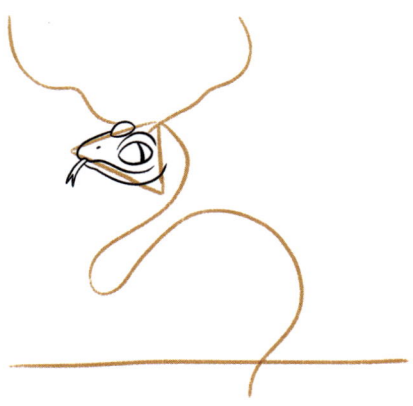

5

Next, we need to sketch where our antlers will go on the Uktena. In this tutorial, we will loosely reference white-tailed deer horns. Above the eyebrow, sketch a curvy antler to the right; to the left of the gemstone, sketch an antler that curls to the left. Each extends to the same height. These lines are the main branches of the serpent's antlers; smaller points will branch off and curve from these lines.

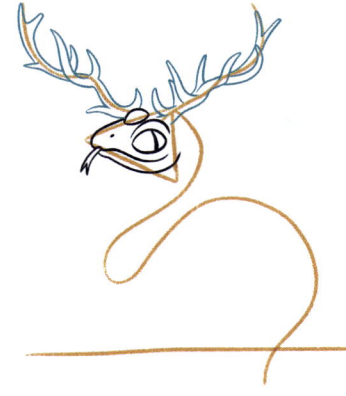

Use your sketch as a guide to draw the antlers. Each antler in this example has eight points.

BREAKING DOWN ANTLERS

Drawing antlers can be tricky! First, sketch the position of each point (in dark brown). Next, consider how they overlap. Draw each layer one at a time.

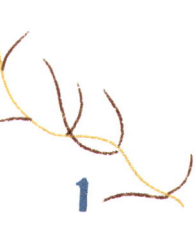

1

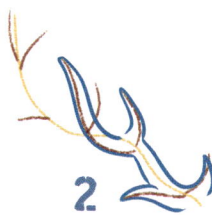

2

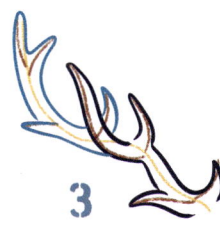

3

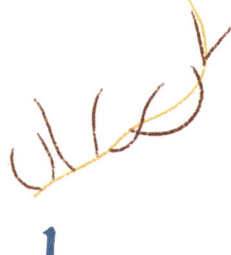

1

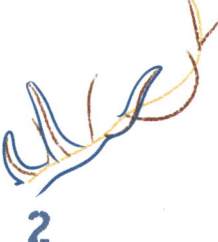

2

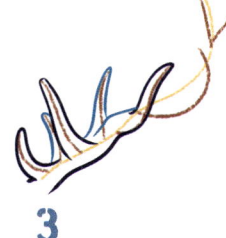

3

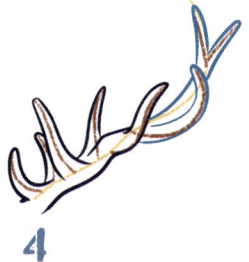

4

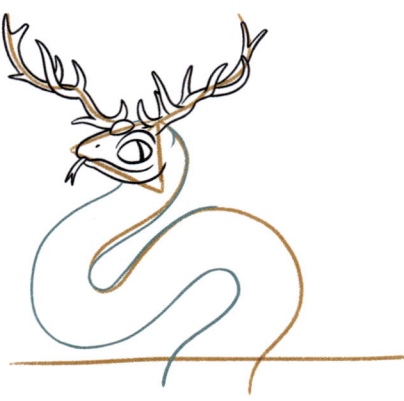

Finish the Uktena's head by connecting the gemstone to the antlers and adding a curve to the right. Leave a gap between the top and bottom of the head. Now, draw its body. Use your sketch as a guide to draw a line that follows its curve, ending at the peak of its arching back. Next, draw the belly.

8

In this tutorial, we are adding wings to the Uktena. Most depictions, however, omit wings. If you want to skip this step, finish drawing the back of the creature by following your sketch and jump to Step 9. On top of the Uktena's back, draw two wings. Each wing begins with a small hump on the back that dramatically curves away. Start with the right wing. This limb opens to the right and is round on top; on the bottom, use sharp ovals or Ws to make the wing feathery. Repeat this for the left wing, drawing it stretched to the left.

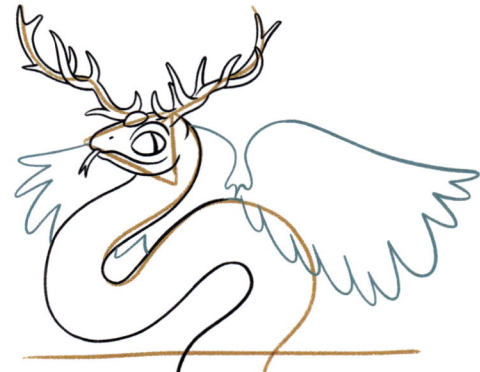

9

Use your sketch as a guide to draw the rest of the Uktena's back. Next, following your horizontal sketch, draw a wavy water line on each side of the snake. Erase your sketch lines.

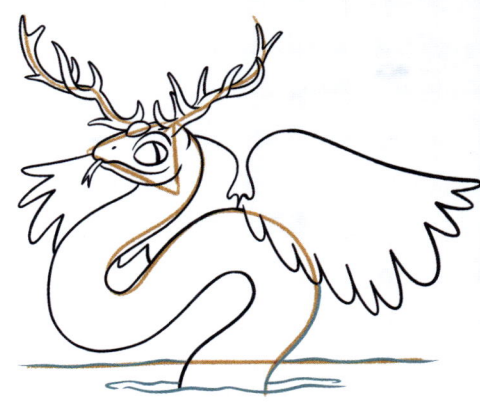

10

If you added wings to your Uktena, add texture to them. Split each wing with a large curve below the rounded portion of the wing. Above this line, draw small, round curves and Ws; below this line, draw taller curves, Ws, and lines that curve with the feathers or angle outward.

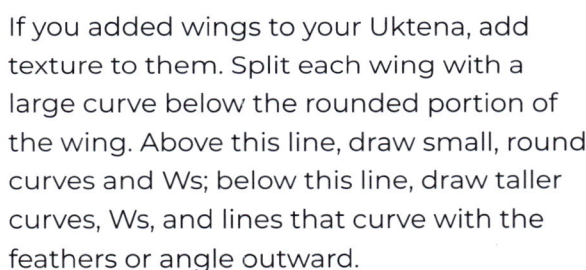

11

To finish, add some final details. First, draw a few lines on the gemstone to give it a geometric shape. Next, scatter scales over the body with tiny ovals and circles. Lastly, draw several wavy, horizontal, and curly lines to show that the Uktena's emergence disturbed the water.

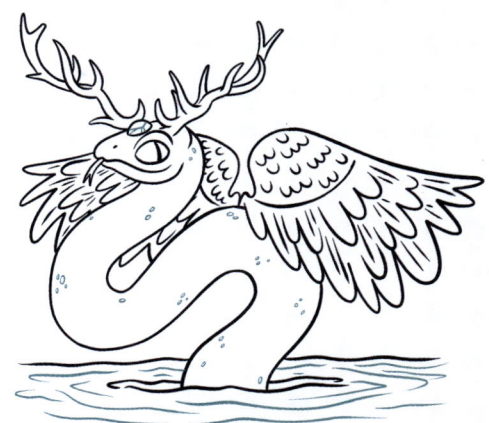

Ogua

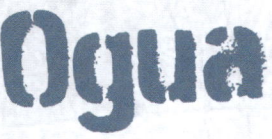

The Ogua is a gigantic turtle that lives in the Allegheny, Monongahela, and Ohio Rivers of West Virginia and Pennsylvania, United States. The large turtle is brown, coated in mire, and sometimes described as having two heads. According to folklore, it can grow up to twenty feet (6 m) tall and weigh up to five hundred pounds (227 kg). The creature is often compared to an alligator snapping turtle, with a spiky shell, long tail, and thick neck. It is said to have a bite so powerful that it can snap a deer in two.

Modern sightings include witnesses recounting huge shadows underwater, blurry photographs, and secondhand accounts. The most infamous encounter originates from the eighteenth century. One sunny day, a family was fishing. With no warning, a reptilian head exploded from the water and pulled the family's son from the shore. With a great splash, neither of them was seen again.

Sketch two circles. The shapes should slightly overlap each other. Next, sketch a semicircle with a flat bottom next to your circles.

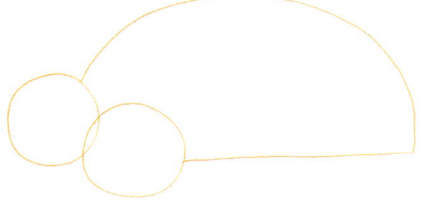

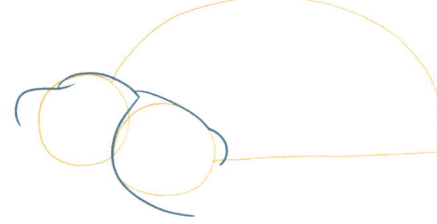

Draw the top of the left head. Below, to the left, add the turtle's snout. Next, draw part of the right side of the turtle's head. To the right of Step 2's lines, draw two downward curves that follow your circle sketch; the left line curves to the right and extends past the sketch, whereas the other line curves to the left and ends with the turtle's round eye.

Draw the turtle's mouths. The left head has a sharp toothy point that transitions into a wide smile. Below it, draw the lower jaw. Then, draw the snout of the right head. It curves from behind the eye to the other side of the head; the snout's center dips down to a point. Below, draw the cryptid's open mouth and thin, bottom lip.

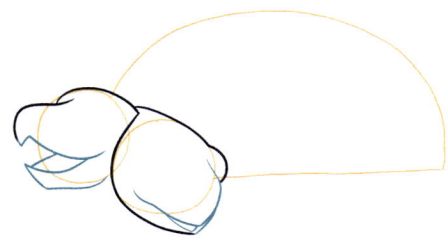

Above and to the right of the turtle's heads, draw the rim of their shell with curving lines.

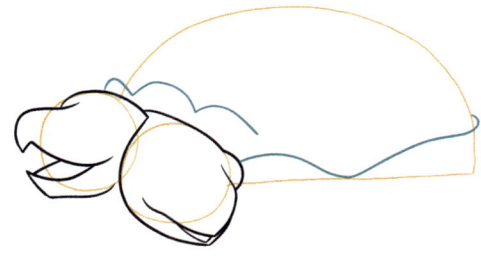

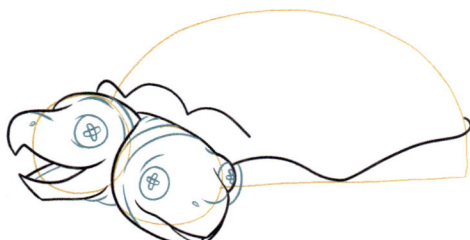

5

Finish the turtle's heads. On the left head, draw an eye slightly above and right of the circle sketch's center. The pupils look like overlapping bandages. Next, add a nostril and curved lines around the eye, on the snout, and left side of the head; then, draw a few more below the head to create a neck. On the right head, draw a few curves of increasing size to create the neck. Draw the eyes and pupils. Afterward, draw a curve above each eye, one on the snout, and add a nostril.

Under the turtle shell, draw two round curves for the front and back legs' knees. Draw a bumpy line for the turtle's belly and inner leg. Next, under the left head, draw a line angled to the left.

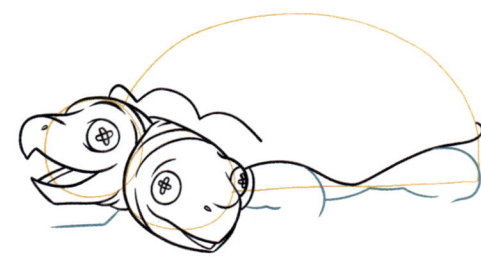

7

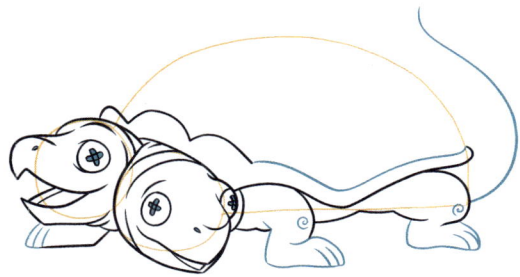

Color in the pupils and nostrils on both heads. Next, draw a line that matches the curve of the turtle shell's rim above it. Then, draw a spiral in the center of each knee. Afterward, draw a foot under each knee and the turtle's left head. Add a long, curvy tail that extends from the back knee and reaches above your semicircle.

8

On top of your semicircle sketch, draw a series of thorns from the shell's left to right rim. Once the shell spikes are in place, draw the tip of the turtle's tail on the right side. Then, erase your sketch lines. Draw more spikes; they should be smaller and their curves wider, being smallest on the left- and rightmost sides.

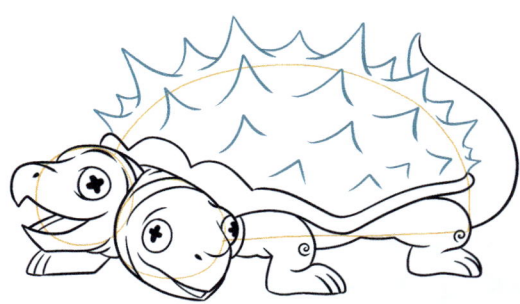

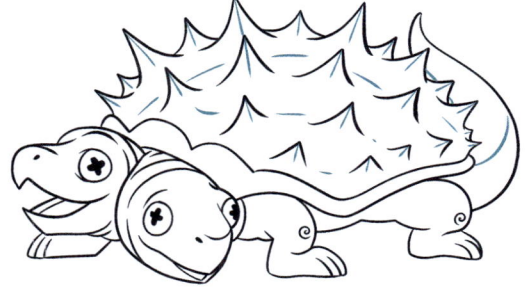

9

Add detail lines to the shell and tail.

TIP

Don't care for this Ogua's spiky shell? Try replacing it with another! While the tutorial is based on an alligator snapping turtle, there are many smooth, bumpy, or boxy shells you can reference instead.

FOREST-CREEPING
CRYPTIDS

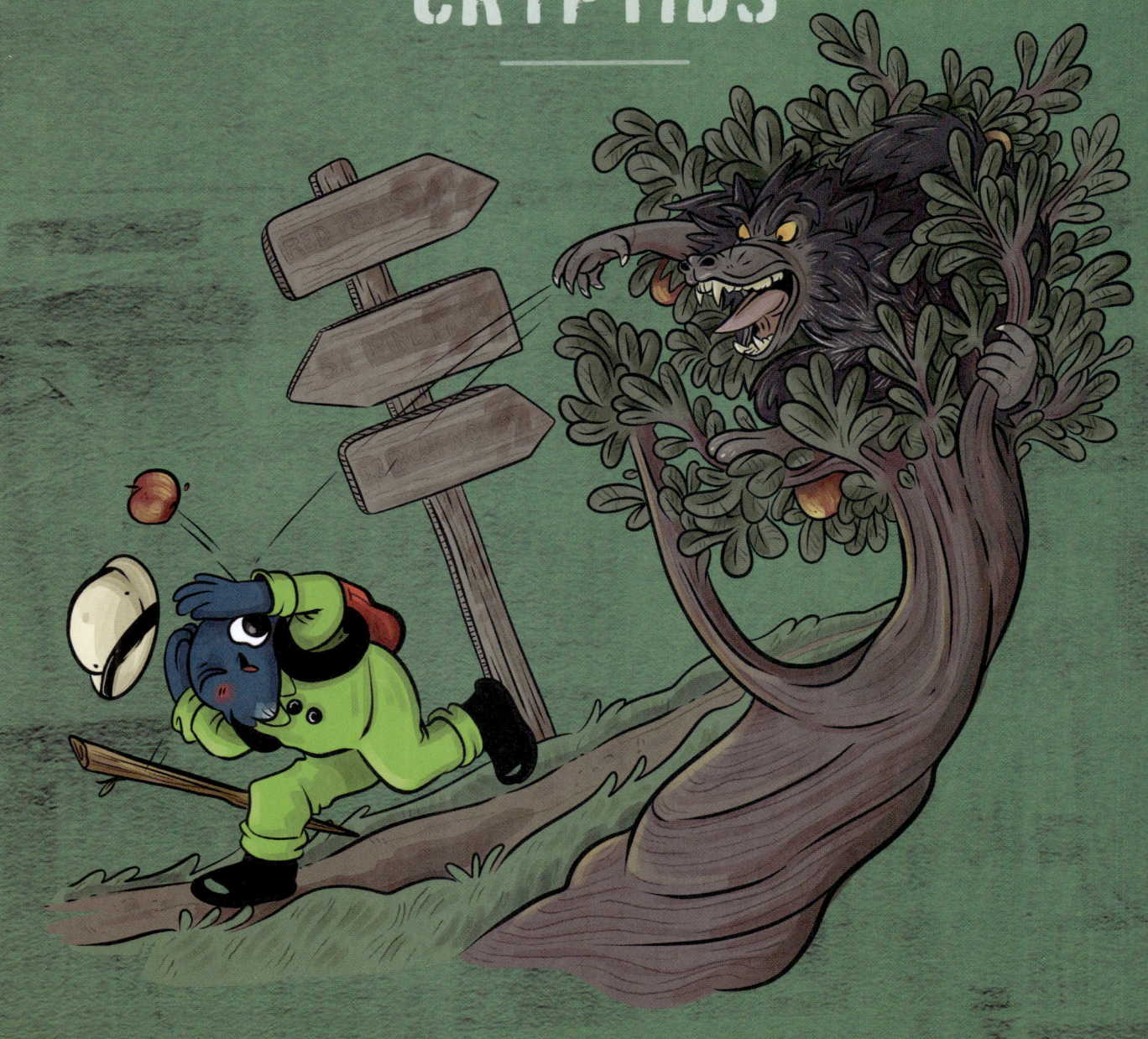

When people think of cryptids, they imagine a strange creature standing in a dense, dark forest. In woodlands, hiding places exist all around—between trees, behind shrubs, in holes, or high in the canopy. While a forest can be fun and pleasant, the same forest can quickly become mysterious or haunting under the right conditions. Cryptids of all shapes and sizes live deep within the woods. Some are attracted to human activity, emerging out of curiosity, annoyance, or hunger; others lure people into the woods or chase them out.

Nandi Bear

The Nandi Bear is a ferocious beast found only in western Kenya. It is a shaggy-haired bear with red or dark-brown fur, long feet, and deadly claws and fangs. Nearly five feet (1.5 m) tall, the highest point of the Nandi Bear is its high-rising shoulders; because of a sloped back, its head and chest appear too big for its body. A carnivore, the Nandi Bear's mouth has pointy, bearlike teeth that can powerfully grip and tear prey. On the animal's otherwise hairless rump is a stubby, furry tail.

Waking after dark, the Nandi Bear is not easily frightened and will attack anything it thinks it can overcome. Standing up on two legs and towering over its prey, the cryptid batters its meal with large paws before eating its fill. According to folklore, when attacking humans, it swipes at the head, tearing off the entire scalp.

1

Sketch a circle. Next, sketch a horizontal teardrop pointing to the right.

2

Draw the ear. To its left, follow your sketch and draw a short, downward curving forehead and a long bear snout. Under the snout, draw the bear's lower jaw; its lip forms a small curl on the lefthand side. Then, use your sketch as a guide to draw its neck to the right.

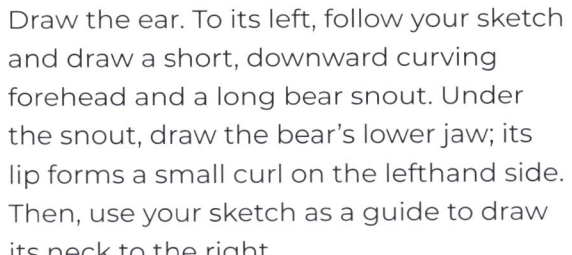

3

Using your sketch as a guide, draw the spiky zigzag of fur on the bear's back. On the left side, the fur curves to the left. As the back rounds upward, the fur will begin to curl to the right. Down the curve of the back, the spikes grow wider. Halfway down the back, draw a wobbly line; near the tip of your sketch, round the line out of your sketch and downward.

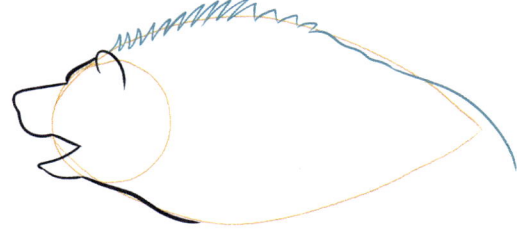

4

To the right of the circle, draw the creature's arm. The left side is a curvy line that almost reaches the top of the back and extends past the neck. Copy this line to the right, but lower. As this line passes through your sketch, curl it to the left, below and past the other line.

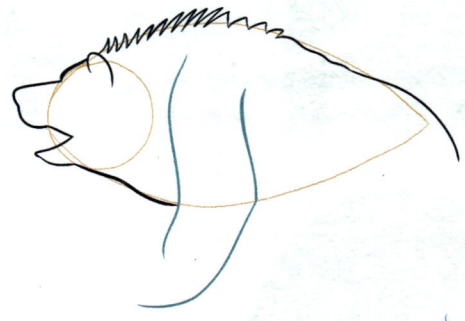

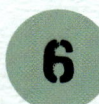

5

Draw the back leg under the right side of the back. Begin with the right line; it is as long as the arm's left side. To the left, draw another curve angled toward the arm; it ends at the same height. Between the arm and leg, use your sketch to draw the animal's belly.

6

Erase your sketch lines. Next, draw a paw under the arm and leg. On the left, the paw is lumpy and comes to an upward, left point. On the right, the paw is pressed to the ground; it has a lump of bunched skin on the top, a smooth, angled ankle, a bumpy bottom line, and its toes come to a left point.

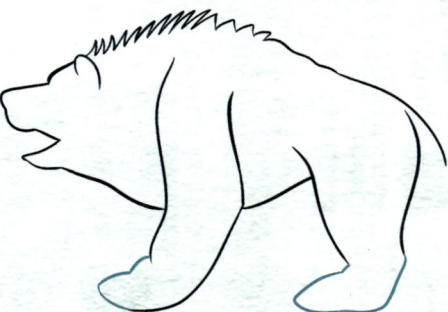

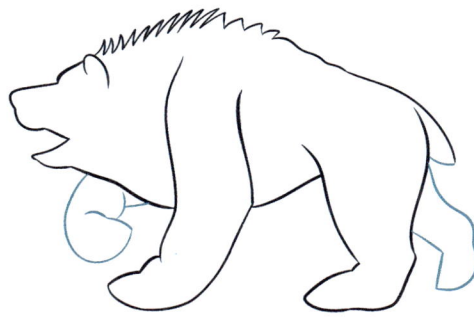

7

Add the tail on the right side by drawing a curve from the back leg. Under the tail, draw the back leg. Then, draw the left front paw under the bear's head. Begin with a round curve that almost forms an oval. Above, add a curve and a diagonal line to finish the arm.

8

Let's add some details, like the Nandi Bear's inner ear, eye, and nose. Create the bear's lips and draw its fangs and sharp teeth. Above the teeth, add a long, curling tongue. Lastly, add five long, curving claws to each paw.

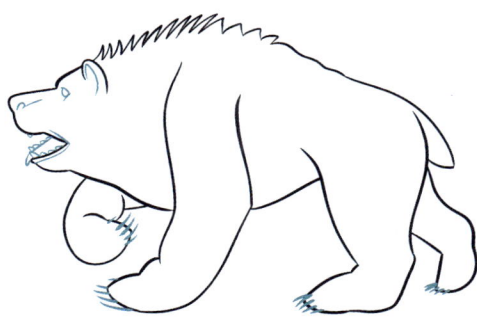

9

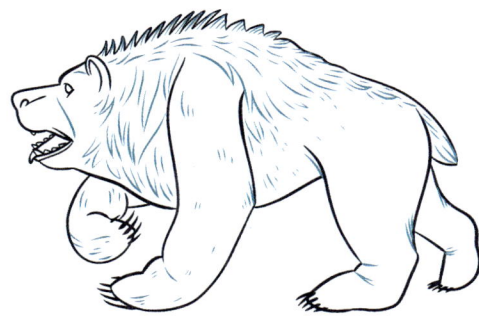

To finish, add texture. Draw wavy, curving lines to indicate fur; match the curl of the fur with how it lays on the body. Lastly, lines should be added where the cryptid's skin bunches and stretches. Add a line where the right arm's paw and each foot bends, and where the hip and back legs stretch.

Squonk

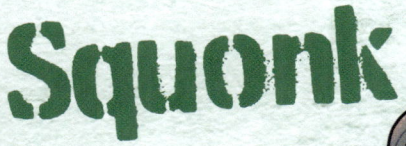

The Squonk is a fearsome critter from Pennsylvania, United States. Small, wrinkly, and believing itself impossibly ugly, it has a pig-shaped body; a human face; and the feet, ears, and tail of an elephant. It is covered in loose, wart-and-mole-speckled skin that hangs in floppy, bunched-up folds. The creature is so self-conscious that it feels only shame and sadness. Unhappily wandering hemlock forests, it incessantly weeps and hides, hoping no one will see it. Unfortunately, its loud crying leaves behind a wet trail, making it easy to find and follow.

Most vulnerable on moonlit nights, the Squonk moves slowly or not at all if there is too much light. Afraid of seeing its reflection on water or its pool of tears, the animal does not look down. If cornered, threatened, surprised, or frightened, the Squonk cries so hard that it constricts and dissolves into tears.

1

Sketch a round bean shape.

2

On the top left of your sketch, create the Squonk's forehead and nose. Under the nose, draw the cryptid's mouth and chin. Beginning with a small curve under the nose's center, draw a deep frown below. To the left, draw two more bumps to add the bottom lip and chin. The lines of the frown and chin should end at nearly the same place.

3

Under the lip, draw a wave to give it a pouty look. Then, draw a tall, thick, triangular tusk on the right side of the mouth; add two curves to show the twist of its lips. To the right of the nose, draw a squished circle with a small gap at the bottom. Within the blank space, draw a tear. Below, add more teardrops running down the cryptid's face. Inside the eye, draw a rounded rectangle for the pupil.

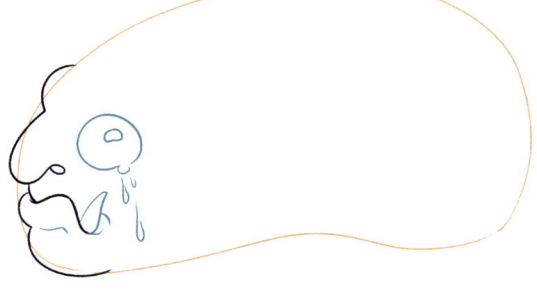

4

Color in the nostril and pupil. Then, draw a lumpy eyebrow above the eye. Connected to the brow, draw a flappy ear like an elephant. Add a few long and short, slightly curved lines inside the ear.

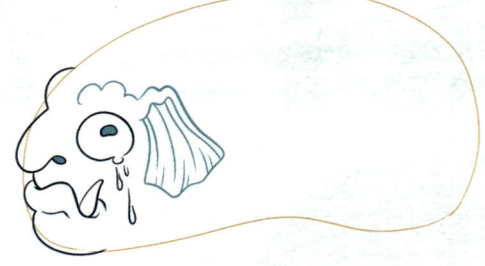

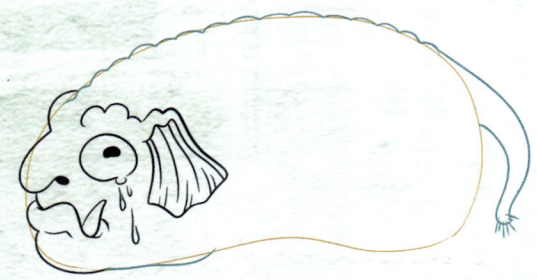

5

Draw the Squonk's back, which is a series of round bumps. Under the mouth, draw the cryptid's jaw. On the right side, give the Squonk a tail. The tail is tapered and ends with a stump and a few bristly hairs.

6

Draw the back leg. Following the curve of your sketch, draw the Squonk's rump; add a rounded angle on the bottom. Across from it, draw an opposite and wider curve; at its bottom, add another opposite curve that nearly meets with the other side. Afterward, draw the wavy line of the belly to the left. Below, add another lower leg; its right side dips inward to show that the appendage is bending.

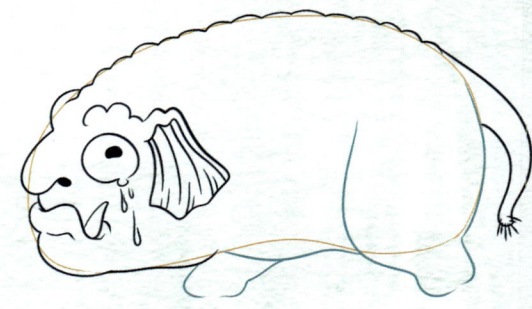

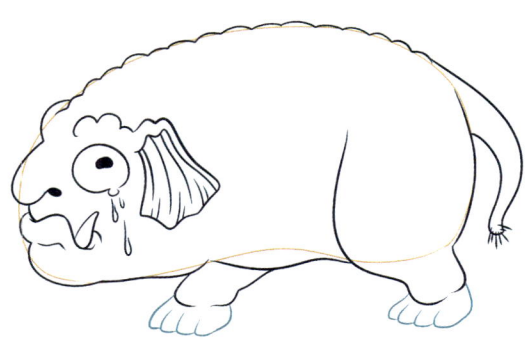

Add feet to the bottom of each leg. Each foot is made up of four slightly pointed curves of equal size.

Erase your sketch lines. Then, draw the back feet.

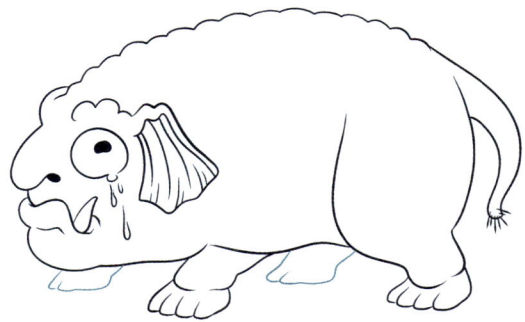

Draw bumps and round curves above and below the eye. To the left, draw the rest of the nose. Draw another curve to the left of the eyebrow, under the mouth, and under the nose. Under the ear, draw a bumpy curve to give the creature a jawline. Next, give the Squonk a lot of texture. Scatter circles and semicircles all over its body in various sizes. Lastly, add round curves on each toe to give the cryptid toenails. To finish, draw its squiggly, bunched-up skin.

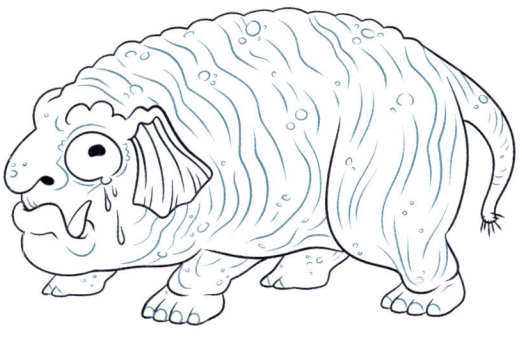

Chickcharney

The Chickcharney, a strange brown, white, and yellow owl, is said to live on the forest floor of Andros Island in the Bahamas. Called one of the ugliest birds in existence, it is both furry and feathery, with wild plumage around the neck and thick feathers all over its body. The creature has enormous, red eyes and a tiny beak. Under its wings hide long, thin, scaly arms that resemble bird feet. At the end of its body is a curled, wispy tail. Flightless, the Chickcharney awkwardly wanders under trees and among brush. Though it stands up to three feet (1 m) on tall, lanky legs, when the Chickcharney senses danger, it hunkers down, blending into the dirt.

According to legend, if one encounters the bird and treats it poorly, they will face tragedy and have bad luck. However, if one is kind to the Chickcharney, they will be rewarded with good luck.

1

Sketch a circle. Add a vertical guideline to the left of the circle's center. Then, sketch a tall oval that touches the bottom left and right of your circle.

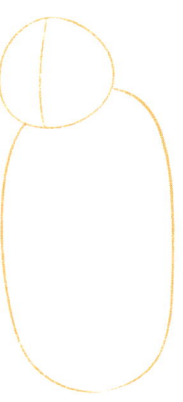

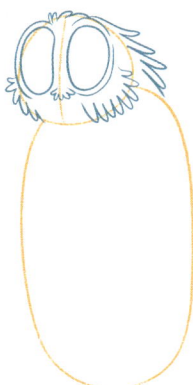

2

Draw two large, oval eyes. Then, on top of the head, draw squiggles that are more vertical at the top, then droop more the farther down the head they are placed. Lastly, draw the cryptid's furry cheeks and a final squiggly line between the eyes; it should look like a small mustache.

3

Under the mustache, draw a tiny beak. Below it, add a round chin. Under that, draw more squiggles and a curve to show the body's transition from head to neck. Add wispy fur around the head. Draw the cryptid's body using squiggly, overlapping lines. Leave the bottom of your oval without squiggly lines.

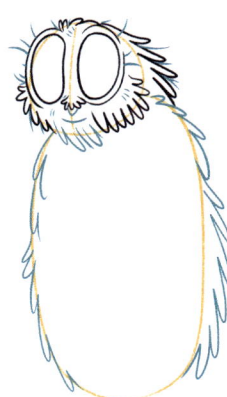

4

Below the head, draw a round curve to the left and right to add shoulders. On the bottom of the bird, draw fluffy feet. Near the center of your oval, draw an upward slope that hooks left at its end and connects to the legs.

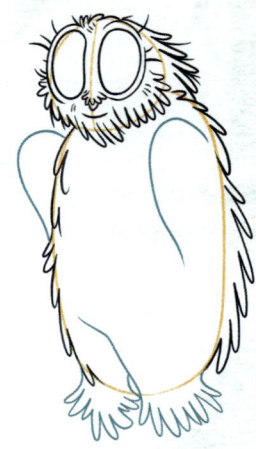

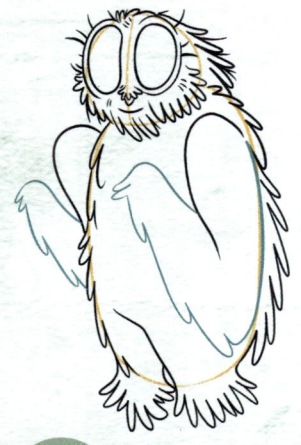

5

Under the curve of the shoulders, draw the Chickcharney's arms. From the left side of each wing, draw an upward curve that rounds at its peak and two long fingers. From the bottom of the hand, draw long, sweeping squiggles that curve down; this line touches the body on the left side and forms an elbow on the right. The right wing's elbow extends upward, tracing the oval sketch.

6

Erase your sketch lines. Under the bird's plumage, add the cryptid's long, sticklike legs. The right leg is held straight; the left is bent at an angle. Each leg has a round ball where the knee is located.

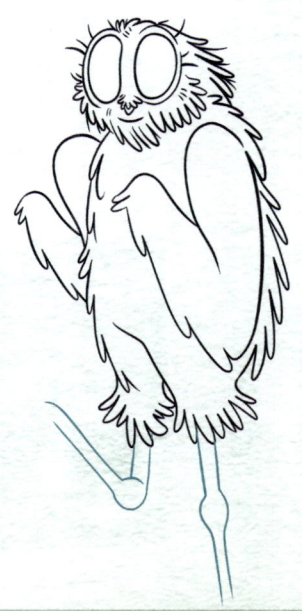

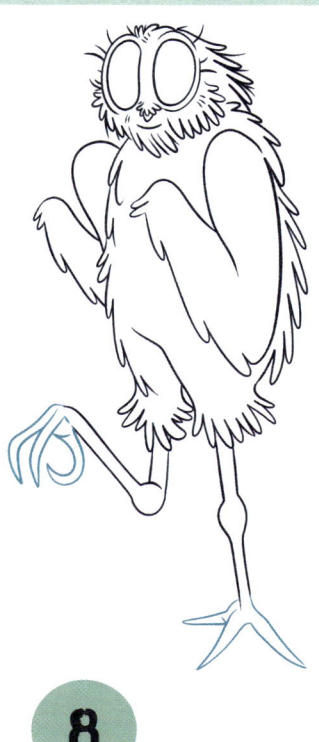

7

Draw the bird's three-toed feet. On the left, the hand is curled almost into a fist. It has two long, thin claws that slightly overlap at the top; to their right, there is a third toe that curls to the left. Lastly, add a small dash and curve for the palm. The right foot is splayed out for balance. Two toes angle outward directly below the leg; a third toe points to the left on the lefthand side. Between the first and second toes, add a dash where the skin stretches.

8

Draw thick, round lines on each toe to create claws. Next, add a curly tail to the bottom right of the figure. Add long, wispy lines to the feathery parts of the bird's outline.

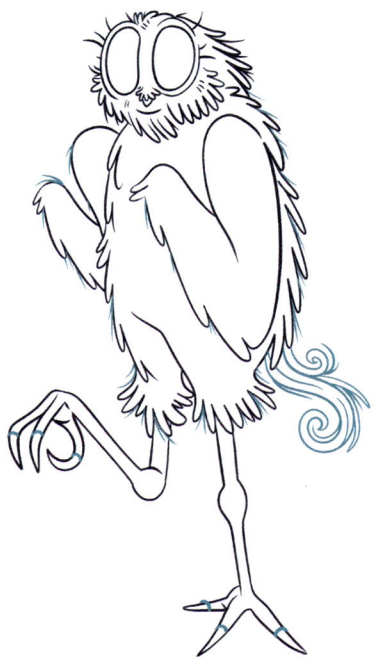

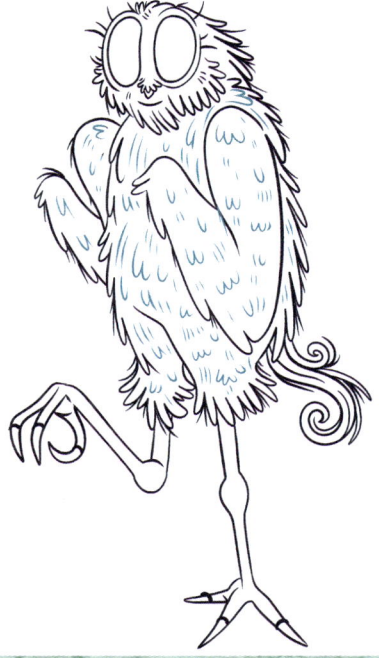

9

To finish, add more texture to its body. Draw several short or long, curved lines, dashes, arches, and Ws to make the bird appear feathery.

Devil Monkey

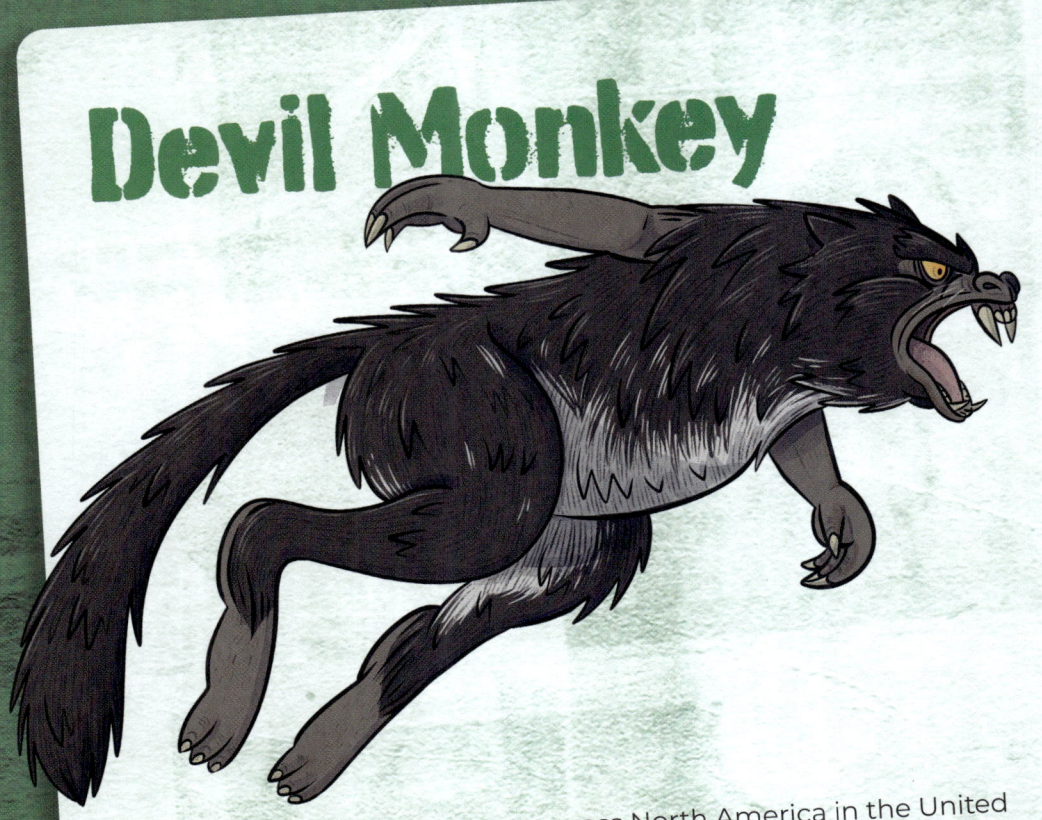

In remote, undeveloped forests across North America in the United States and Canada, terrifying baboon-like creatures make homes among cliffs and rock piles. Standing three to four feet (1 m) tall, Devil Monkeys are aggressive primates that are very different from Sasquatches. Covered in shaggy brown or black hair with white streaks and bellies, Devil Monkeys are muscular with short arms and a long, bushy tail. Their faces are doglike, with long snouts; small, furry, pointed ears; and prominent, protruding canines. Having legs like a kangaroo, Devil Monkeys are confused for the marsupials—*until they move*. According to eyewitnesses, these primates can jump with incredible speed and distance; one witness saw one leap over a twenty-foot-long (6 m) field.

Devil Monkeys are dangerous and violent. They have scratched, bitten and ripped roofs from cars, killed livestock, and attacked pets.

1

Sketch a circle. On the top left of the shape, sketch a downward, curvy line. This will be the Devil Monkey's head, back, and tail.

2

Draw a jagged, zigzagging line from the top right of your circle to past the edge of your sketch. This line creates the furry outline of the creature. Then draw a left-pointing, flattened ear on each side of the head. Draw spiky pieces of fur around the face.

3

Draw the nose and left nostril under the fur on the righthand side. Below, draw the Devil Monkey's outstretched maw. Add its bottom lip and a round chin. Back to the snout: Draw a line to the left that follows the curve of the mouth. To the left, draw another, similar, but shorter line; above and attached to it, draw a round curve to the left. Afterward, draw a short curve next to the snout that nearly joins the mouth and top of the head.

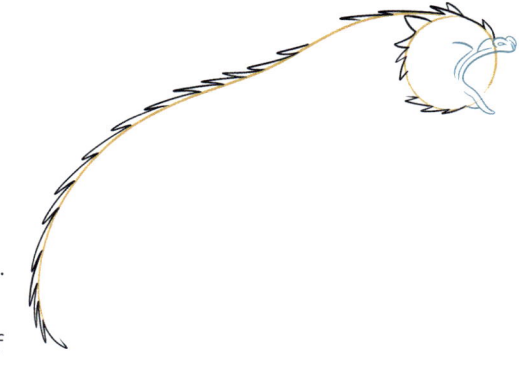

4

Draw a furry eyebrow at the top right of your circle. Below, draw the cryptid's eye. To the left of the cheek, draw two sharp points of fur. Between the bottom lip and chin, draw a small curve.

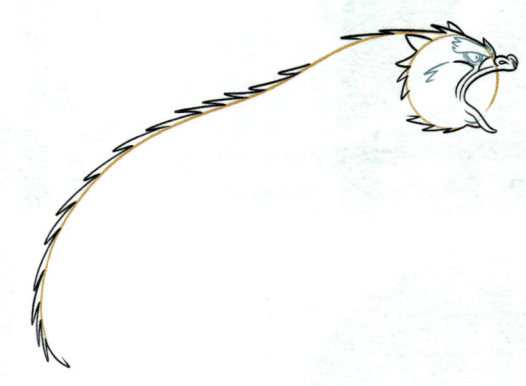

5

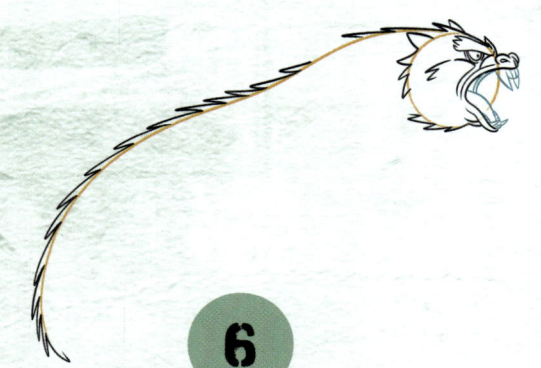

Under the snout, draw the cryptid's mouth. The inside of the mouth contains teeth and sharp fangs.

6

Erase your sketch lines. Under the Monkey's back, draw the back leg. Start with a broad curve; the line should curl to the right at the top and slope left toward the tail at its end. Add a rounded, zigzag of hair. Next, draw its neck and belly. Under the belly, add the other leg. To do so, draw a spiky, curving line; to its left, draw a short curve in the opposite direction.

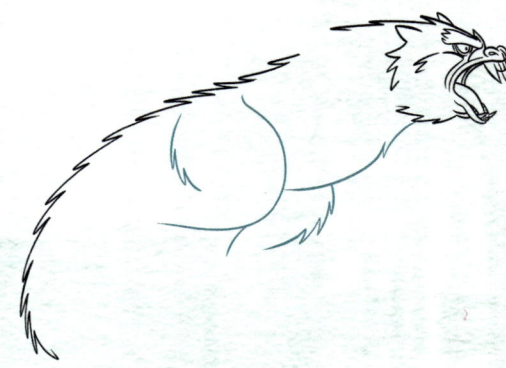

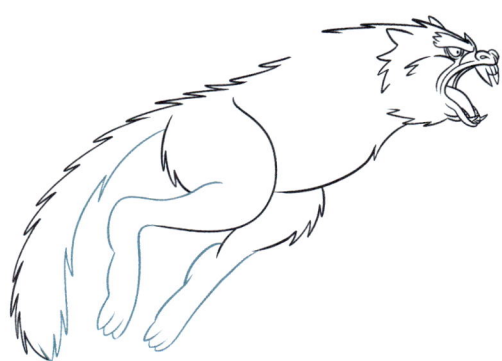

7

Finish drawing the left leg by adding a curvy line to the left. Then, under each leg, draw one of the Devil Monkey's kangaroo feet. Draw the furry bottom of the tail.

8

Add the Devil Monkey's arms. Use curved spikes to draw the hands.

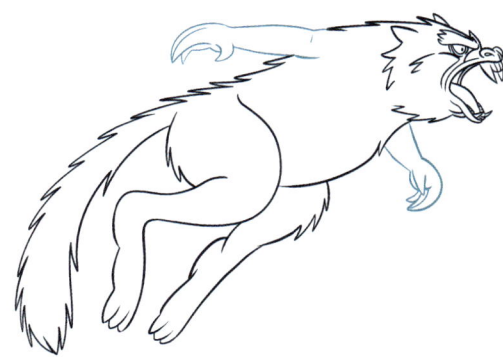

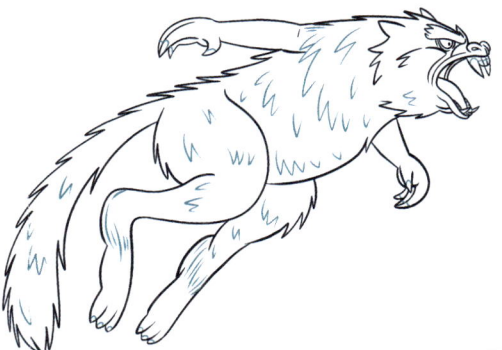

9

To finish, add a few details. On the creature's top teeth, add gum lines. Then, add finger and toenails. Lastly, give texture to the Devil's Monkey body.

TIP

To draw the Devil Monkey in another pose, follow the Chupacabra's tutorial (page 29), replacing its features with that of the Devil Monkey. The two cryptids share many similarities, making the Chupacabra a great base to draw from.

Unicorn

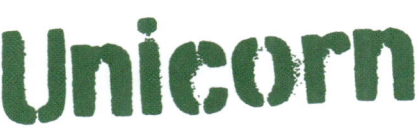

The unicorn is a cross between a horse and a goat. Contrary to its appearance, the animal is incredibly aggressive and deadly. Its most notable feature is one long, large, and sharp spiral horn on its forehead. According to legend, this horn (called the alicorn) has many medicinal and magical qualities. If ground up and mixed with various ingredients, it can cure ailments and diseases, provide protection from illness, detect poisons, purify water, and even revive the recently deceased.

Unicorns were accepted as real up until the 1400s. Unicorn artifacts made by tricksters can be viewed in museums; the objects are made of walrus tusks or narwhal or rhinoceros horns. While most people firmly disbelieve the Unicorn ever existed, cryptozoologists are unsure. In fact, some believe that the animals, due to their horns, were hunted to complete or near extinction.

1

Sketch a triangle pointed to the left and tilted downward. Above and on top, sketch a diagonal line. Below, sketch a right curve on the rightmost corner of the triangle. Then, sketch a left curve left of the triangle's center; both lines are the same height. Underneath, sketch a small hill.

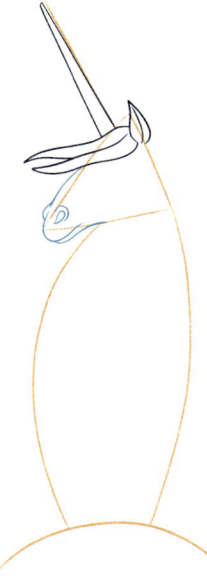

2

On the top right side of your triangle, draw the Unicorn's ear and a few wispy tendrils of blowing hair. Then draw the Unicorn's horn: a thin triangle whose tip is round instead of pointy.

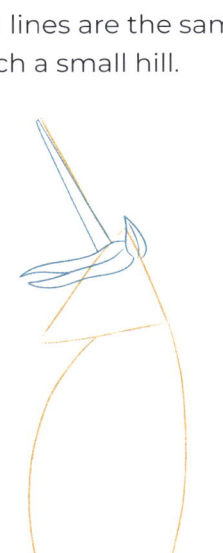

3

Add the Unicorn's snout. Extending from under its hair, the nose is a downward curving, round shape; on the snout's tip, there are two nostrils, one on the outer edge, and the other inside the shape. The snout transitions into an unimpressed frown. Below, add a thin chin.

4

Begin drawing the Unicorn's luxurious mane. The left side of the mane is comprised of curvy triangles, as the hair is blowing in the wind. The mane on the right side is also wavy but draw only its smooth edge for now.

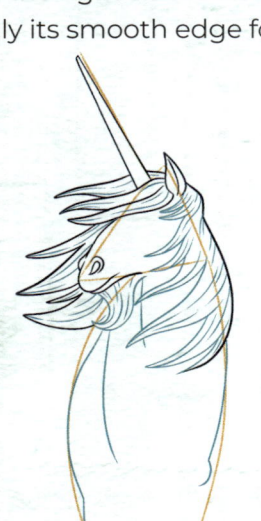

5

Finish the Unicorn's mane and beard. Add texture to the hair with curving lines of varying size that follow the direction of the mane or beard. Then, draw the Unicorn's neck. Afterward, use a series of curved lines to add more details to the Unicorn's body.

6

Draw foliage over the top of your sketch under the horse. Creating grasses or a bush, use bubbly round lines and curves that overlap each other. Afterward, extend the lines of the left and right legs to your foliage. Erase your sketch lines.

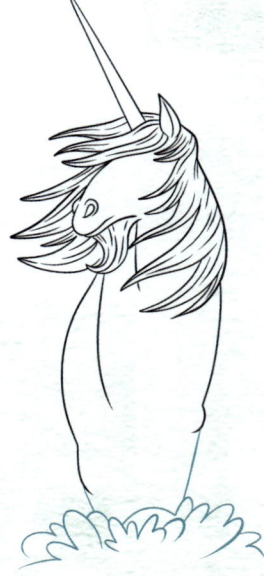

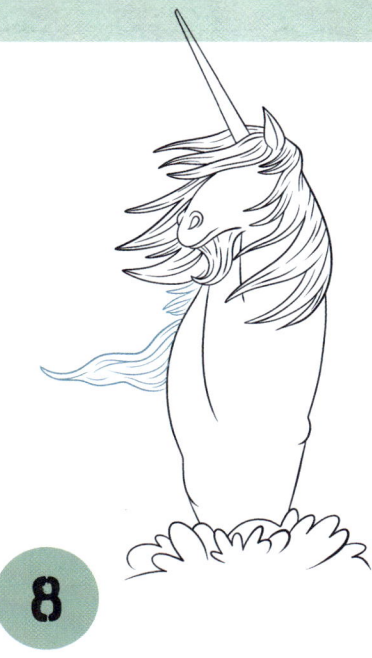

On the left side of the Unicorn, draw the final strands of the creature's mane. Underneath, draw the tail. Inside the tail, add texture lines that follow its curve; most should extend from the base of the tail.

8

Finish drawing the outer left front leg that you started in Step 6. In the center of your horse, finish drawing its legs. Below the neck, draw a V with a flat bottom. On each side, draw an inner leg by mirroring the outer legs and tapering the limbs. The knees' curves should reach at least the center of each leg. Between the two front legs, add a back leg and a small, diagonal line for the horse's belly. To the left, finish the other back leg, mirroring the outer leg lines.

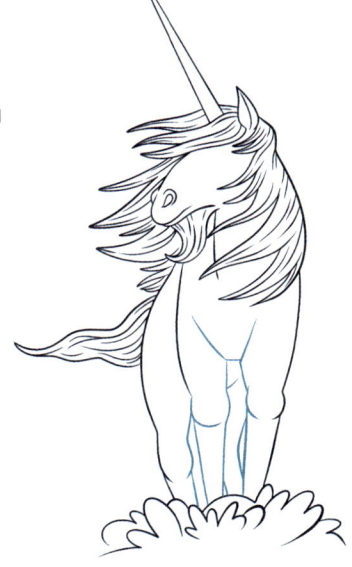

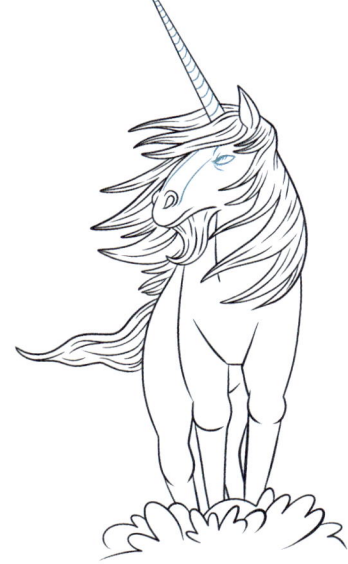

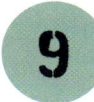

To finish, add details to the Unicorn's horn and nose. Lastly, draw the creature's eye.

NIGHT-SEEKING
CRYPTIDS

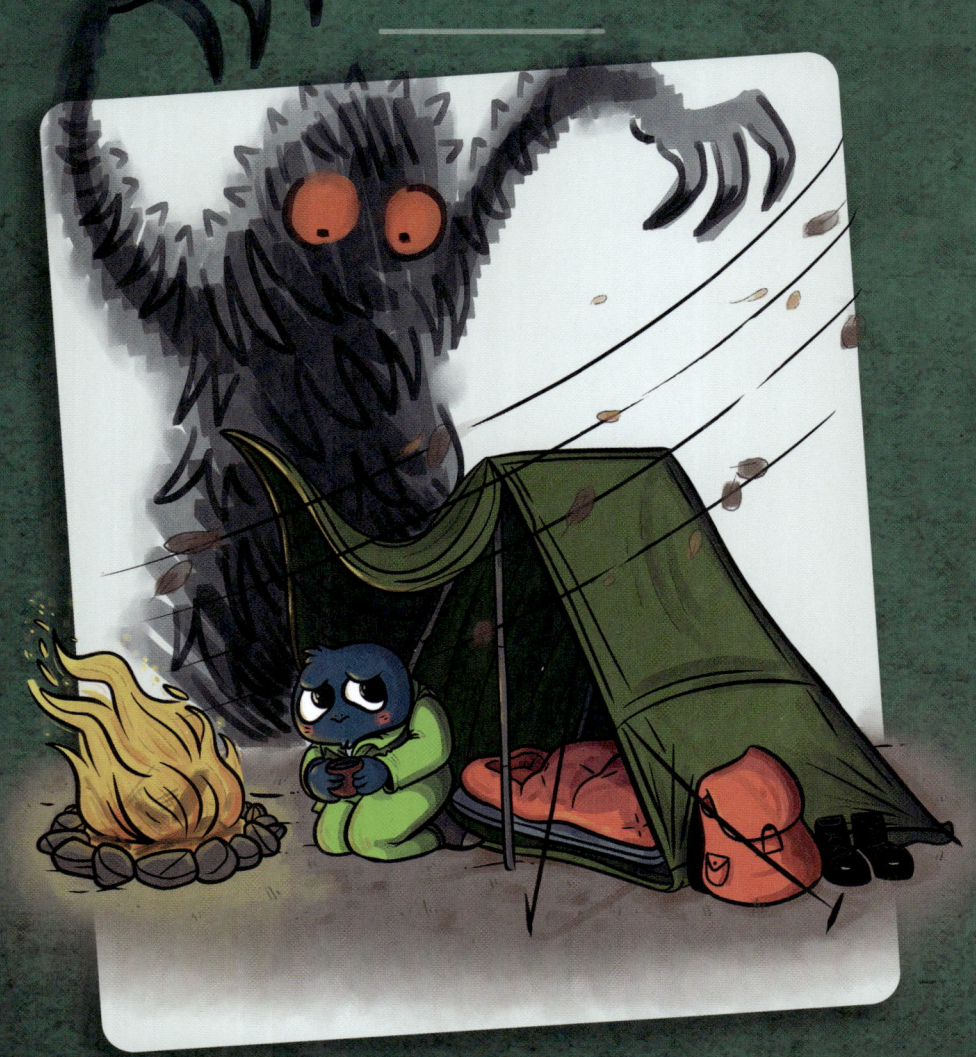

Some animals sleep during the day and are only awake at night. Called nocturnal, several cryptids fall into this category. Like many nocturnal animals, almost all nighttime cryptids are considered scary. In all fairness, most *are* malicious and indiscriminately hungry. Adding to their creepiness, nighttime cryptids often follow their victims, leaping out and surprising them when they least expect it. Nocturnal cryptids are most notorious for their horrific sounds: shrill screams, guttural snarls, high-pitched cackles, and sinister whispers are a few associated with the cryptids featured in this chapter.

Hopkinsville Goblin

On August 21, 1955, the police station in Hopkinsville, Kentucky, United States, received a panicked family of twelve; they claimed to have been visited and attacked by aliens. Their farmhouse was soon invaded by police officers and the military. According to the family, a spaceship descended from the sky bearing four small creatures. They had large, pointed ears, small legs, shiny skin, and glowing yellow eyes. The beings tried to break into the home, pulling at doors, peering through windows, and scratching at the walls. Each time the aliens came into view, the family shot at them.

Several investigations were conducted on the property, but the only evidence recovered were bullet holes in the windows and doors. The family packed up and left the next day.

1

Sketch a circle. Below it, sketch a rectangle.

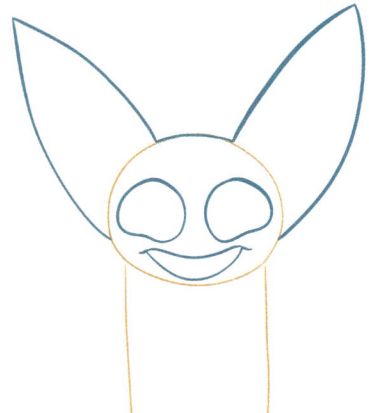

2

At the top of your circle, draw two large, pointed ears. Between them, trace your sketch. Then, on each side, draw two large, bean-shaped eyes. Below, draw a grin; on each side, the lip rounds up into a smile.

3

Above the eyes, draw two downward angled eyebrows. On the outer edge of each eye, draw a curve. Under the eyes, draw two dashes on the cheeks. Between the eyes, draw two nostrils. Lastly, draw the goblin's bottom lip, then the bottom of its head.

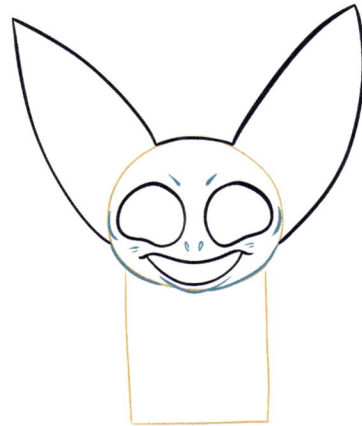

4

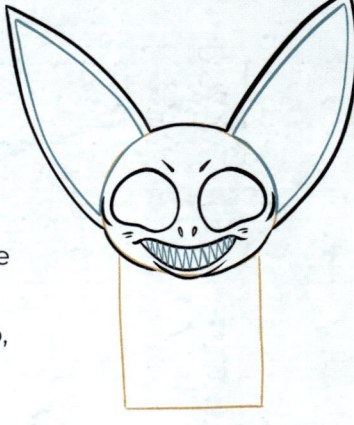

Finish the ears; copy their shape inside and trace the circle. In the mouth, draw a zigzagging line to create sharp, little teeth.

5

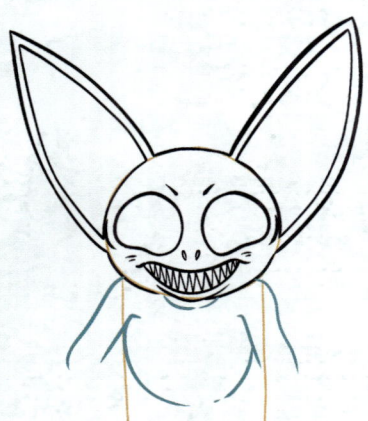

Draw the alien's upper arms. Each limb extends from below the head and is angled outward; the arm dips inward on the outer line and, on the inner line, angles inward at the top. Draw the neck below the head with two curves. Between the arms, add a round belly that almost comes to the bottom of your sketch.

6

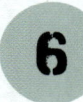

Draw the forearms and wrists; they are angled oppositely from the upper arms and reach the bottom of the sketch. On the outer side of the arm, add a curve.

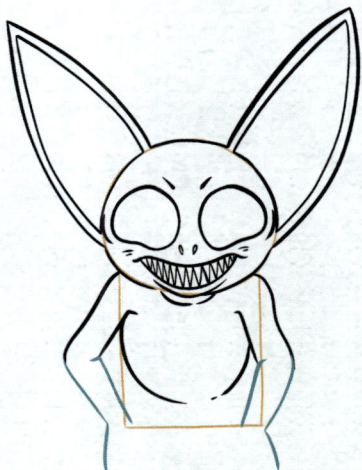

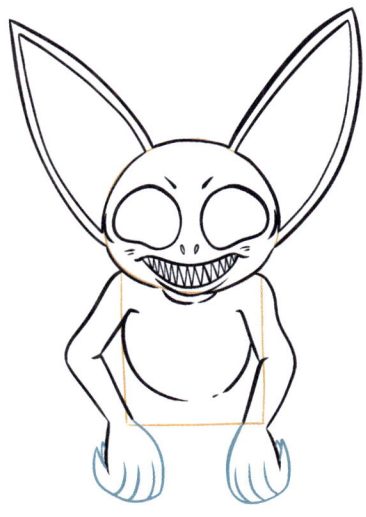

7

Draw the hands. On the inner arms, add a curve longer than the one drawn in Step 6; below each, draw an outward-curving line that ends with a sharp claw and attaches to the palm. Add another claw between them and their palms. Then, draw three curved lines on each hand.

8

Sketch the Hopkinsville Goblin's legs. Like a crescent moon on its side, the legs form two thin, bendy triangles.

9

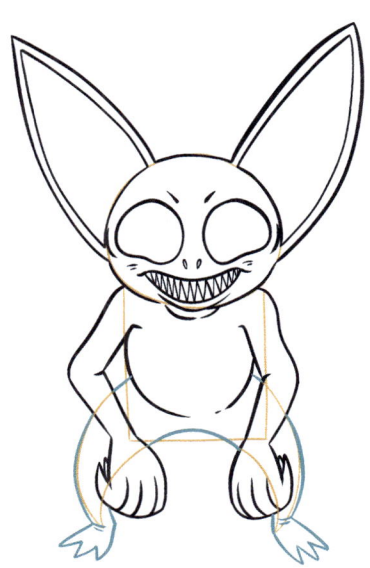

Use your sketch as a guide to draw the visible parts of your sketch. Do *not* draw the bottoms of the sketch, though. Instead of bringing the shapes to a point, add feet. Each foot is a wedge shape with three spikes pointed away from the body. Where the leg meets each foot, draw two small curves. Erase your sketch lines.

Hellhound

Hellhounds are malicious, large, black-haired dogs with one or two glowing red or yellow eyes found in England, Wales, France, and the USA. Taking slightly different forms around the world, they are dangerous beasts that may breathe fire, be encapsulated by flames, or have fiery eyes. Many have an incredible or supernatural ability. This talent may be great strength or unmatched speed; some can speak, turn invisible, pass through solid objects, or fly.

Hellhounds are associated with death and unpleasant afterlives, and in some cultures, looking into the eyes of one is enough to secure your immediate demise. Alternatively, hearing the dog's howl or simply seeing it at night may bring death. These cryptids are also linked with unpleasant, overwhelming odors like sulfur, rotten meat, and burnt hair. Hellhounds frequently encountered in a region are often given a unique name. The one seen in the British Isles, for example, is called Black Shuck.

1

Sketch a thin triangle pointing to the left. Below it, sketch the curving line of the Hellhound's neck and back. Above, sketch two tall, pointy ears. The left ear will be smaller, thinner, and float above the head.

2

Draw the right ear, making it sharp at the top and curvy on the sides. To the right, draw the neck; below, add a hump for shoulders. To the left of the ear, draw the forehead and snout above your sketch, ending on the triangle's leftmost point. Below, curve around the point and end the curl on the triangle's bottom line.

3

Next, draw the thinner left ear, connecting it to the forehead. Then, draw the inner ears. Add two small lines where the forehead meets the snout. Draw a nose and a nostril on the end of the snout; add three dots to the right. Under the snout, draw the bottom lip.

4

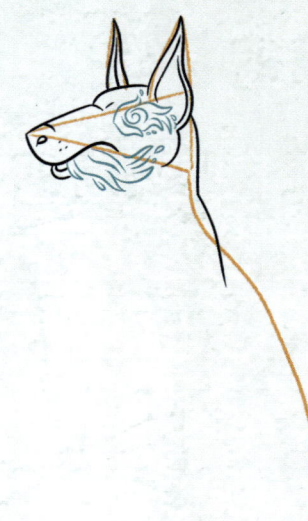

Now, give the Hellhound a fiery eye and breath! In the open space under the mouth, draw a burst of flame escaping its lips with wavy lines, curves, and angles. Add smaller shapes or lines at the end of the flame burst to show the fire dissipating. Use the same types of lines and shapes for the eye. Begin in the center of the eye with a swirl.

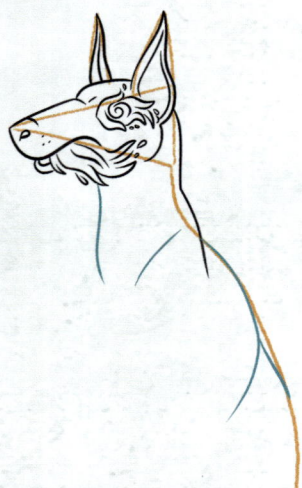

5

Below the mouth's flames, draw the curve of the neck. To the right, draw the muscular curve of the shoulder. On the dog's back, trace your sketch, but transition to a downward, left curve, ending it under the shoulder. To the right, add another curve that meets back with your sketch.

6

Draw the animal's right arm below the right shoulder. Afterward, draw the chest with an angle from the upper arm to the left side of the neck. Bisect it with a line that nearly meets with Step 5's neckline.

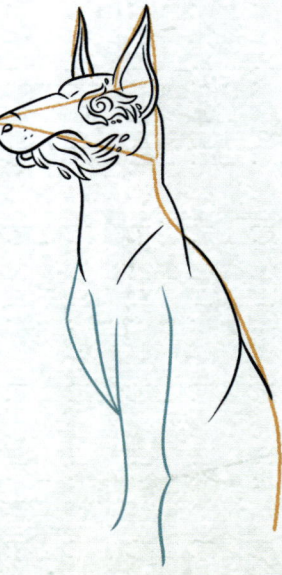

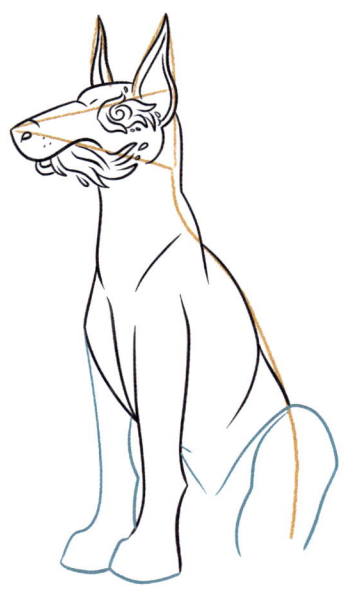

7

At the bottom of the arm, draw a blocky paw. Next, below the leftmost point of the cryptid's chest, draw the left arm as you did in Step 6. At the bottom, add another paw. In the empty space at the bottom of your sketch, draw the right leg. Near it, a second diagonal angles upward, forming a V shape. Add another small diagonal above. Below the knee, draw a curve that dips down near its center.

8

Erase your sketch lines, then draw the rest of the legs and paws. Lastly, sketch the tail by adding an S at the bottom of the right leg. At its end, sketch an arrow pointing away from the dog.

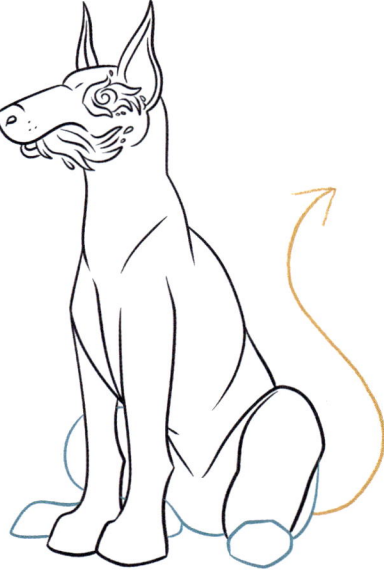

9

Divide each paw with curving lines to create toes. Use your sketch as a guide to draw the tail; it should be thicker at its base. At the tip of the tail, angle outward to meet the sketch of your arrow. Then, trace the shape. Erase your sketch lines.

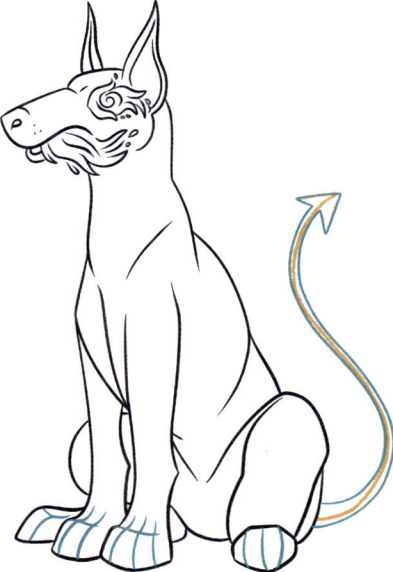

Kentucky Goatman

In Louisville, Kentucky, United States, a satyr has made a home under the Pope Lick Creek train trestle. Part goat, part man, it has a hunched body with dark, greasy hair, pale skin, and short, spiky horns between its ears. A bipedal, the clop of its hoofs may be heard late at night near the bridge.

First documented in the 1980s, many still believe in and search for the Goatman, though no evidence of the creature has been recovered. Unfortunately, six people have died and two have been injured exploring the trestle. The railway has issued precautions and threats to potential visitors of the dangers of climbing the railway, even adding a tall fence posted with warnings.

1

Sketch a thin, downward pointed triangle. Extending from the top-right point, sketch a curve that dramatically dips downward and rounds to the right.

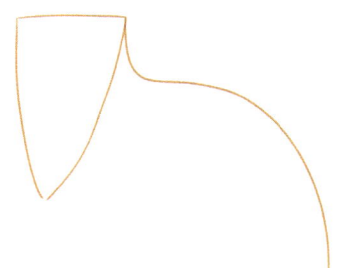

2

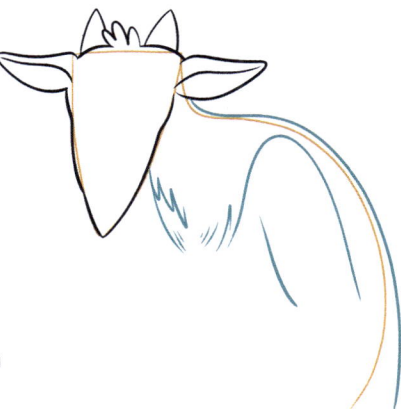

On top of each side of your triangle, draw two outward-pointing goat ears. Below them, use your sketch as a guide to draw three slight, outward bumps for the eye, cheek, and fluffy beard on each side of the head. Between the ears, draw the top of the head, a squiggly line of fur, and two small, triangular horns.

3

Under the right ear, use your sketch as a guide to draw the cryptid's back. To the left, draw the soft, zigzagging line of the neck. Then, to the left and right of the neck, draw curving lines of fur. Under the peak of the back, draw the right shoulder with a tall arch and a downward slanted line.

TIP

Some stories claim the Kentucky Goatman carries a large, rusty ax. Find reference images and try drawing the creature wielding one!

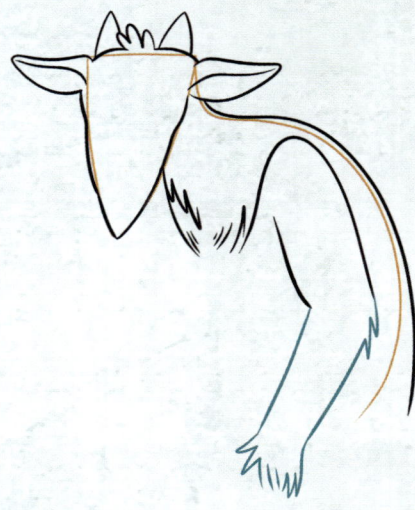

4

Draw the right arm under the shoulder. Angled to the left, the limb has furry points on the elbow and at its bottom.

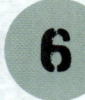

5

To the left of the arm, draw a leg with its knee raised, below the chin. Like the arm, the leg has furry points on the knee and at its bottom. The leg ends slightly below the height of the arm.

6

Under the arm, add a fist; on its right side, draw a small pinky finger. At the end of the back, draw a goat's tail. Then, draw a curve from below the knee to the tail, skipping over the hand.

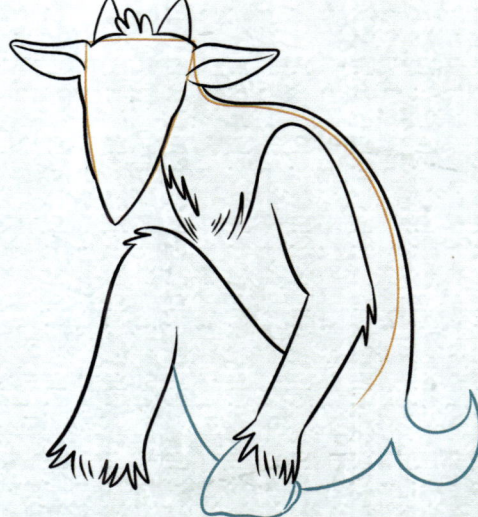

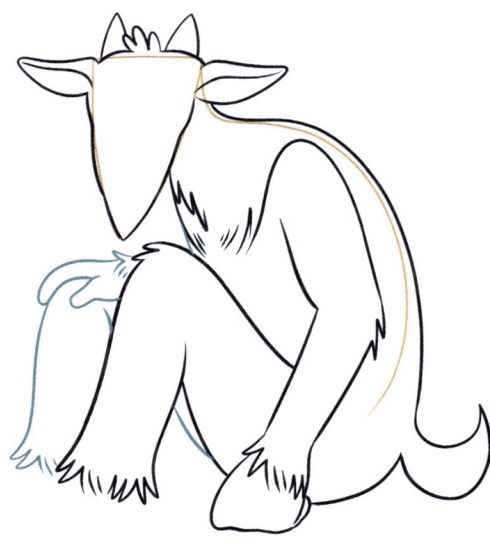

7

To the left of the knee, draw a hand; resting on the other leg, only the thumb and first finger are visible, curling around another knee. Below the hand, draw a leg like in Step 5; add a curve under the right leg. Add a short line on the left side of the chest.

8

Add the Goatman's hooves. Then, add texture: Draw the inner ears, add curves to the horns, fingernails to the left hand, and lines of fur all over the body.

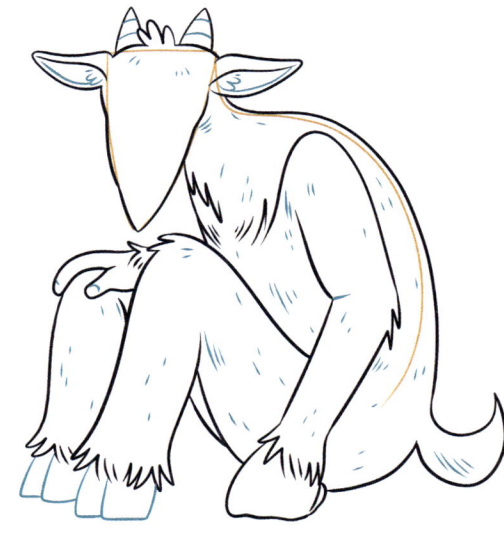

9

To finish, draw the face. In the middle of the head, draw a curvy, furrowed unibrow. Below its center, draw the nose and mouth. Then, draw an eye under each side of the eyebrow. Inside the eyes, draw and color in a bent, rounded rectangle. Under each eye, draw a round curve. Lastly, draw curved, vertical lines on the beard.

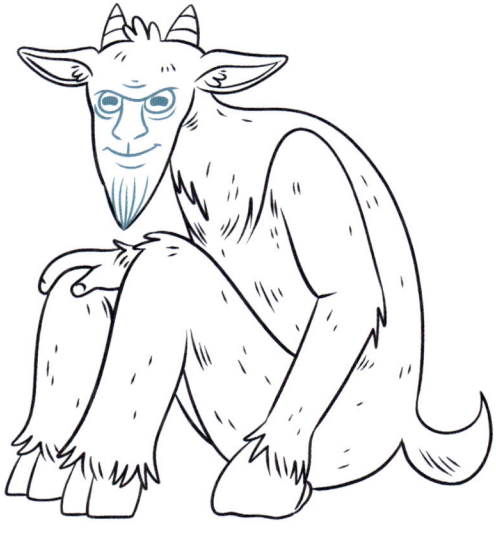

Pale Crawler

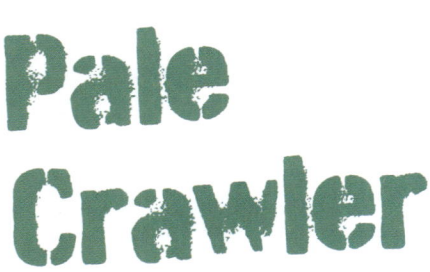

Pale Crawlers are monstrous creatures caught on security footage and trail cams. Lightly colored, they appear as hunched, nude figures that walk on all fours. Skeletal, their bodies seem frail and stretched thin. While their eyes are dark voids when observed in person, they shine white or green when viewed on-screen.

Pale Crawlers are experts in stealth and camouflage. Able to skulk a foot (30 cm) or less away without being detected, they watch and follow people. Living in dense, remote woodlands, abandoned homes, or derelict tunnels, they make beds of trash and debris, eating whatever they can catch. While curious about humans, they still eat them, attacking victims in their homes while they sleep. The creatures are smart and can open doors and windows, as well as slip through tight spaces.

1

Sketch an upside-down teardrop. In its center, sketch a vertical guideline and a curved horizontal guideline.

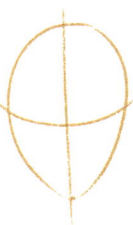

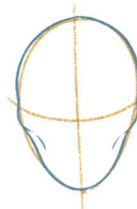

2

Use your sketch as a guide to trace the outer edge of the shape. Below the horizontal guideline on each side of the face, draw a round cheekbone that curves inward. Below, curve the line inward before continuing to trace the sketch; add a curve inside each side to make the cheeks appear more sunken.

3

Draw a hooked curve on each side of the head. Next, draw the cryptid's eyes above your horizontal guideline. On the inner side of each eye, draw the bony nose's curve and a second, outward curve below. Between the lines, draw a sharp triangle where the guidelines meet.

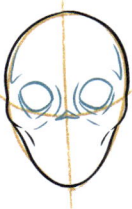

TIP

To make the drawing scarier, stretch the Crawler's mouth to an unsettling, unnatural length. You can also tilt the creature's head or add more bone and skin texture.

4

Draw the mouth with a curvy, round shape that is narrower at the top. Inside the mouth, draw teeth on the top and bottom. Curve the overall shape of the teeth to match the lips' curves. Between the bottom teeth, add a tongue.

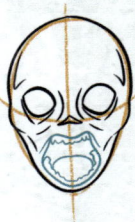

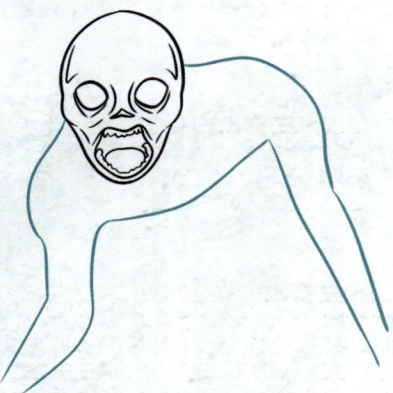

5

Erase your sketch lines. Draw the shoulders; as the creature is leaning to the left, the right side's lines are longer. Between the shoulders, draw the chest's horizontal curve. Below each shoulder, draw the monster's long, thin arms.

6

Add curves around the inner elbows, neck, shoulders, and chest. Below the chest, draw the creature's torso. In the center, add two downward diagonals to create the waist. On the left side, draw a bony curve and add the bent, left leg below.

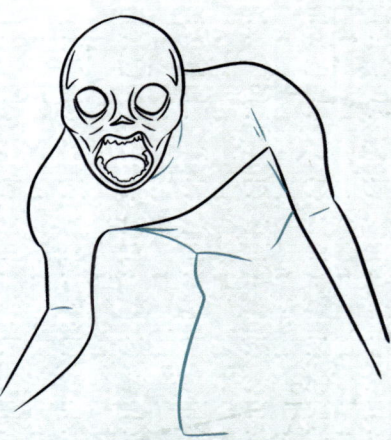

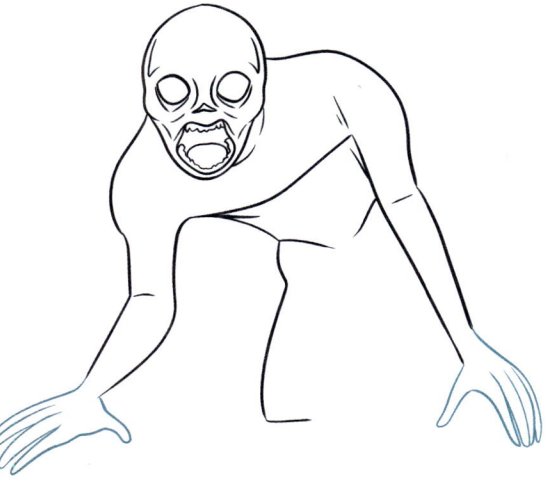

7

Next, draw a hand under each arm. Each hand has five long, bony fingers. The left hand is held against the ground and pointed to the left; its thumb curls to the right. The right hand hangs down with its fingertips resting on the ground; each finger overlaps and the thumb points to the left.

8

Under the waist, draw the legs. Draw a tall arch that extends from the right hand's thumb and ends above the left leg's knee; the left side of this line has a curve to the left. Draw a knee between the right hand's fingers and an ankle behind them. Under the left side of the arch, draw the tapering, left leg.

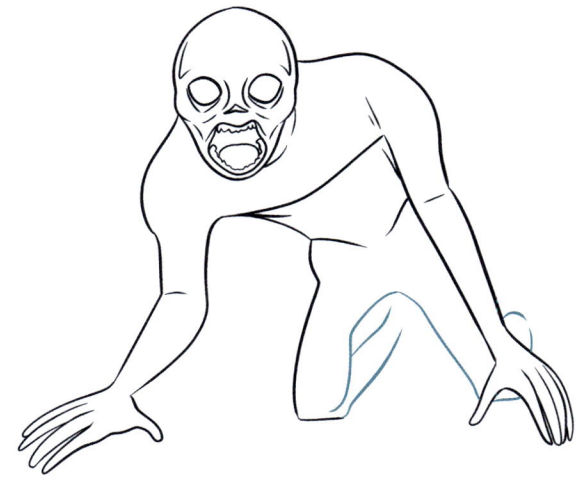

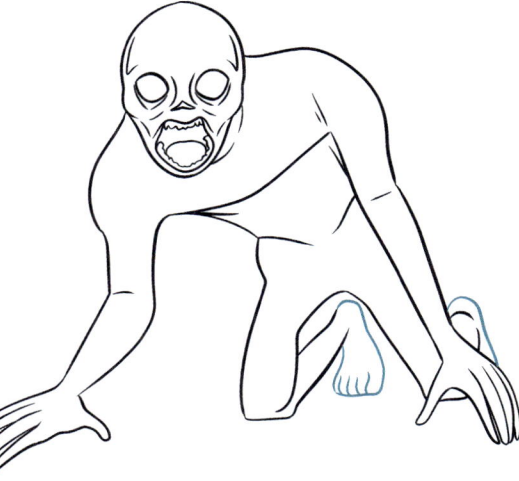

9

Lastly, draw the feet. The right foot is a continuous curve above the ankle. The left foot is wedge shaped; it is round at the top and squarish at the bottom. Inside this foot, draw four short, wavy lines to make toes.

Jersey Devil

In the Pine Barrens of New Jersey, United States, a bizarre monster has haunted the forests for hundreds of years. Having the head and body of a horse, the horns and legs of a goat, the tail of a demon, and the wings and arms of a dragon, the creature is an amalgamation of many animals.

The monster was blamed on eighteenth-century Pines Barren resident and suspected witch Mother Leeds. While in labor pains with her thirteenth child, she cursed and dedicated it to dark forces; born hairy, winged, and completely inhuman, it escaped and ate children for the next fifty years.

Sightings of the cryptid have never slowed. Originally called the Leeds Devil, in the twentieth century, it received its name, the Jersey Devil, coined by the newspaper that reported an alleged attack on trolley cars in New Jersey. Today, it is treated as a state mascot.

1

Sketch a triangle pointed to the right.
From the top left, draw a downward,
left-sloping line.

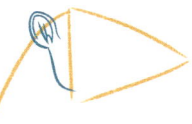

2

Draw the cryptid's round ear in the space
between your triangle and line. Then,
draw the inside of the ear. Below, add the
monster's jaw.

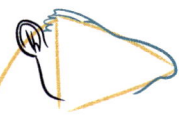

3

To the right of the ear, draw a squiggly line
of hair that rounds the triangle point. Above
it, copy the line. Below, use your sketch as a
guide to draw the Jersey Devil's snout; it has
a round, droopy end.

4

Draw a nostril on the snout's tip. Below, draw the top teeth, a thin chin, and the bottom lip; color in the inside of the mouth. Below the ear, draw a line that matches the curve of your sketch but flares toward it at the bottom. To the left of the mouth, draw the cryptid's bottom jaw and neck; include a few points of shaggy fur in the line and copy the curve of the upper neck.

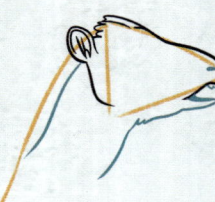

5

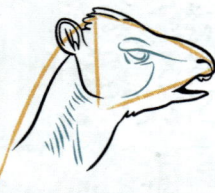

Toward the bottom of your triangle, draw a round cheek that hooks left. Above, draw the long, curving line of the eyebrow that nearly touches the nostril. Above, add a small curve. Below, add a triangular curl for the eye. Under the eye, draw a similar line that touches the brow and loops below and past the eye. Add a final mark to the left of the eye. On the neck, add furry texture: Draw a series of curved lines behind the jaw and a few others lower on the neck.

6

On top of the head, behind the ears and fur lines, draw the horns. To create these wide, curling cornucopias, draw a shape that curls upward and to the right, coming to a rounded point. Draw the left horn first.

7

Draw the wings. Beginning with the left wing, extend the line of the neck with a tall, tight, upward arch that transforms into a rounded point at the top. From there, draw a long, sloped line to the left, stopping over halfway down your sketched line. Veer right, drawing a sweeping downward angle. Make a thin, slightly curled point at the end of the wing, then connect it to the top. Between the wing and the head, draw the tip of the back wing.

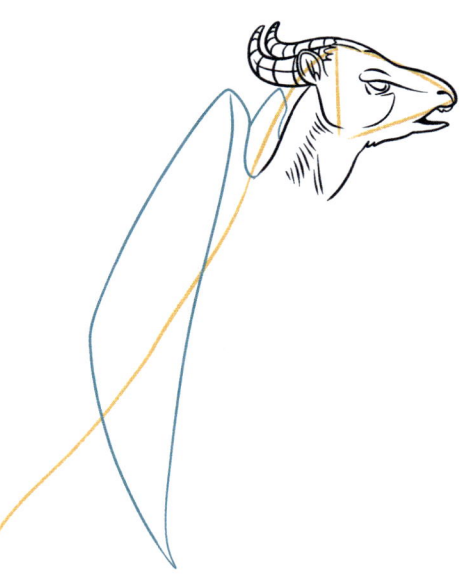

8

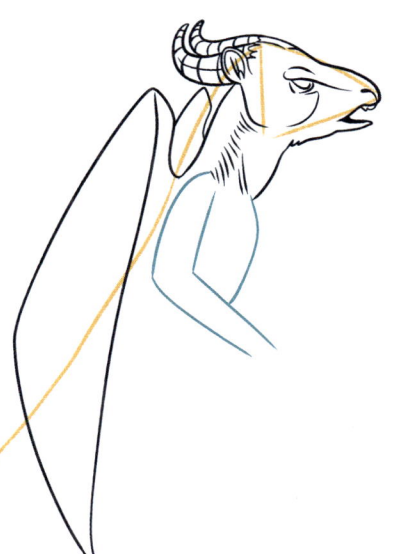

Near the neck's furry texture, draw an arm. The limb has a round shoulder; its forearm angles to the right and tapers slightly, reaching below the eye. Afterward, draw the chest between the arm and neck, connecting the two.

FUN FACT

The Leeds's family crest (a batwinged dragon called a wyvern) is thought to be at least partial inspiration for the Jersey Devil's appearance.

9

Draw a three-clawed hand at the end of the arm. The palm is round, and one claw sticks out to the left. Above the arm, draw a second wrist and hand. It is smaller than the previous hand; on it, draw an angular thumb and long, right-pointing claw. Below, add the tips of two claws. Under the left arm, draw a stretched S shape to create a leg. To the left, draw the back leg with a slanted line. To the right, draw another curving leg under the hand; the knee grazes the leftmost claw. To the right, draw the leg's underside from the left leg's knee.

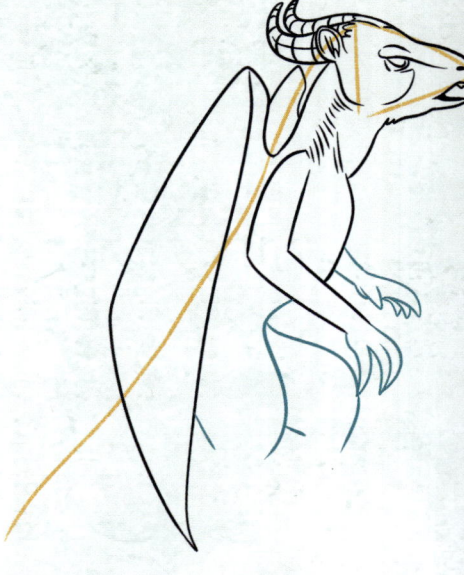

10

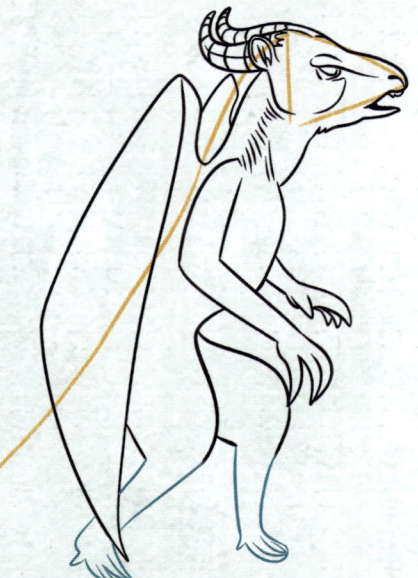

Under each knee, draw the lower legs. Thin, tapering shapes, each leg ends in curling points of hair to the right and one hair spike to the left. The left leg is bent at an angle, whereas the right leg is held straight.

11

Between the left arm and wing, follow your sketch and draw the creature's back. Then, behind the wing, use your sketch as a guide to draw a thin, forked tail. Lastly, draw a hoof under each leg. Each hoof has a round bump on the upper left and a flat bottom. Each side of the foot is curved, the right side more so.

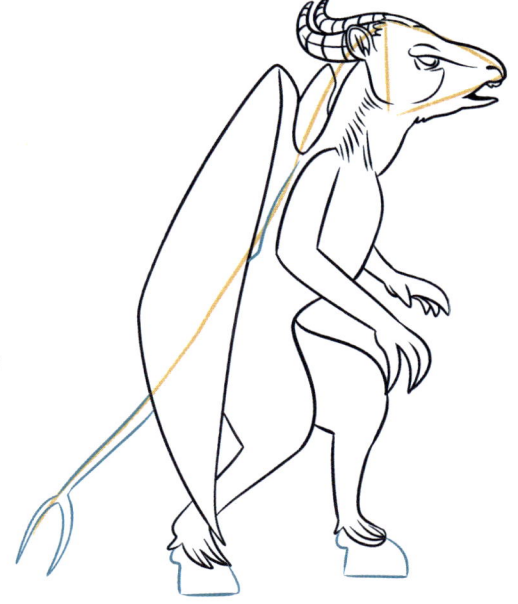

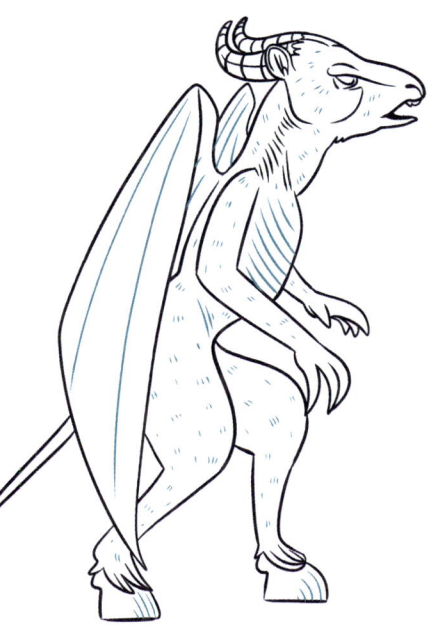

12

Erase your sketch lines. Add texture by drawing small dashes of hair over the monster's body. On the chest, draw a series of long, upward-curving lines to make it appear gaunt. Above the left leg, draw a few curving lines. On each wing, draw a few long curves that almost touch the top and bottom of the wing and curl slightly to the right. Don't forget to add a few on the left wing's underside. Lastly, add a few round lines on each hoof.

Not-Deer

Seen throughout the Appalachian Mountains is an animal that looks like a deer but slightly *off*. Usually its jerky, stumbling movement is noticed first. Like the gait of a newborn deer, the creature's unusually long legs are double-jointed and bend at unsettling angles. Barrel-chested, it balances on four sticklike legs. Called the Not-Deer, its eyes are what is most frightening to witnesses. Positioned on the front of the head instead of the sides, these wide eyes convey emotion and great intelligence.

Unafraid of humans, the Not-Deer approaches people; it cannot be easily run off, spooked, or outsmarted. Standing up on two legs, it walks toward witnesses and swings its forelegs threateningly. If onlookers are not scared away, the creature drops to all fours and rams them with its horns or chases them up trees or off cliffs. The Not-Deer is often hidden among herds of deer at night.

1

Sketch an oval. Down its center, sketch a vertical guideline that curls to the left.

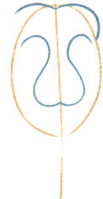

2

At the top of your oval, draw the deer's forehead with an M-like shape. To the right of your guideline, draw an S; the top should almost touch the forehead, and the bottom should rest on the guideline. Reverse the S to the left of your guideline. Both lines should reach the same height and end at the same point, creating an upside-down heart shape.

FUN FACT

Some people believe Not-Deer are caused by regions polluted by radioactive waste. These renditions may depict them with a third eye, mangy fur, or other signs of illness.

3

Under each arch, draw an eye; the inside of each should touch the snout. Copy the eye's shape inside each eye to create a pupil. Above each eye, draw an inward curve that reaches toward the eyebrow; below, draw another curve. Then, above the point of the snout, draw a triangular nose with a curve to split it into two. Draw a curve under the snout's center to give the creature a lip. Next, draw bumpy lines on the left and right sides of the head to form cheeks and a chin.

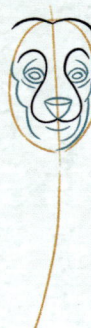

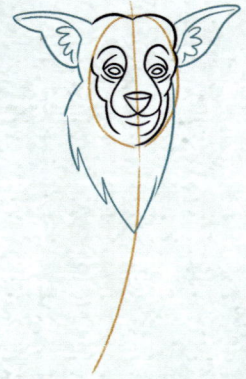

4

On each side of the forehead, draw a large, pointy ear. Afterward, draw the inner ears and their fuzzy centers. Below, finish drawing the head and neck; the left side is indented near the eye and the right side extends from the right cheek. The neck ends in a zigzag of triangular-shaped fur.

5

Draw a sloping shoulder on each side of the neck. The right should be straighter, but the left should be longer. Draw a sharp zigzag of fur on the left arm's elbow. Above, draw the inner arm below the furry neck.

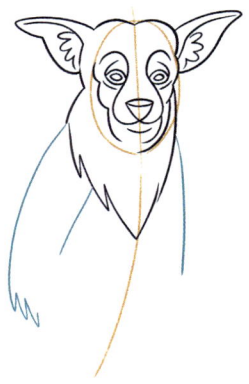

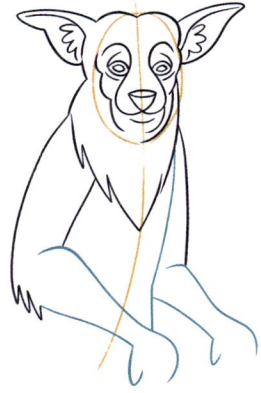

6

Draw the forearms. Beginning with the left arm, draw a thin, tapering shape from left to right; the upper line is a very round line. To the right of this upper line, draw a round wrist; on the lower line, add an upside-down arch. Above the arm, draw the curving, vertical line of the chest; the line is indented near the bottom. Afterward, draw the right arm. Repeat the steps used to draw the left arm on the right side of the body. This arm should be slightly smaller than the other, as it is a little farther away.

7

Add hooves to the arms. Each hoof has curving lines of hair at the top and two overlapping, rounded triangles below. Underneath, draw the upper legs. Each leg line is the same height. The leftmost leg has two oppositely curved lines, one connected to the back, the other angled toward the back at the top. The right leg extends from the left hoof.

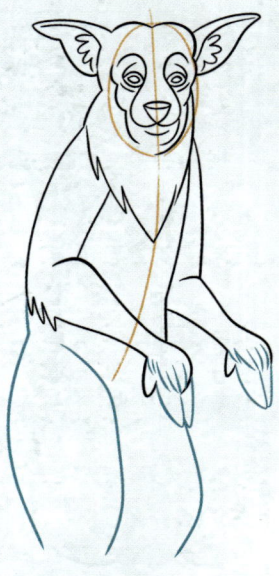

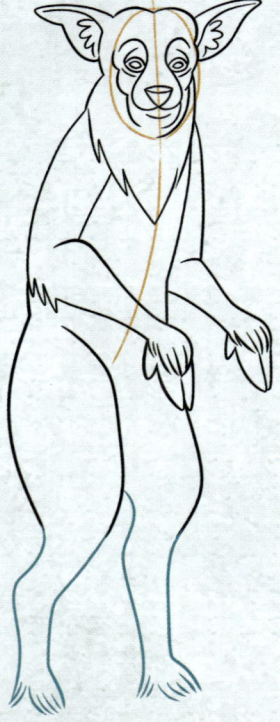

8

Next, draw the lower legs. Each limb curves to the left and forms a round ankle; the limbs then go straight down and end with curvy lines of fur. The left leg is more bent than the right, so it is curvier, whereas the right leg is longer. Flair the left side of each leg outward at the end.

9

At the bottom of each leg, draw a hoof. These are shaped similarly to those drawn in Step 7, though larger, longer, and more horizontal. In the middle of each foot, draw a curved line through the center. On top of the head, sketch the Not-Deer's antlers. The bottom line is the main branch; it is a wavy line that faces away from the creature. Above and attached to it are five antler points. Some overlap with each other.

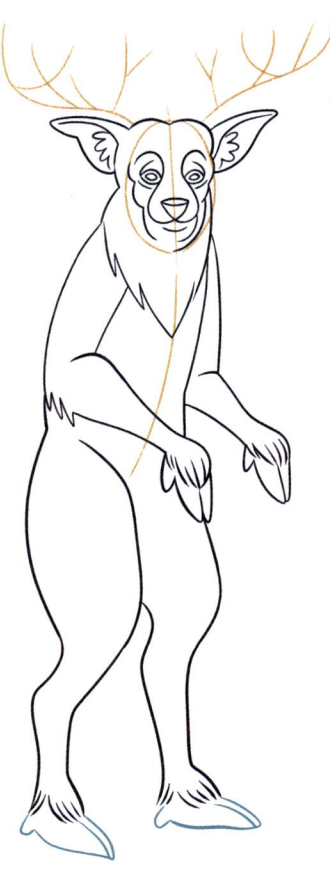

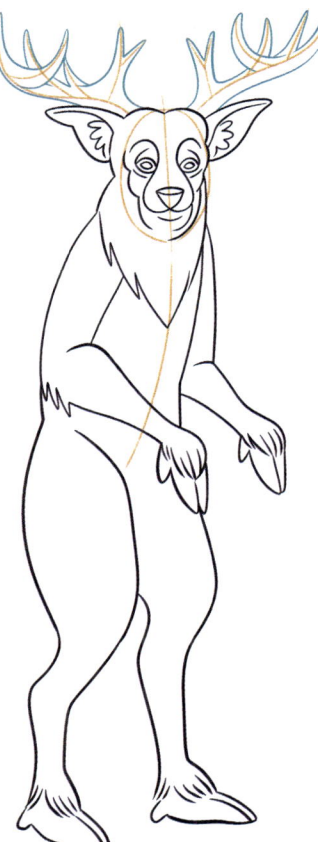

10

Use your sketch as a guide to draw the antlers. For the left antler, draw the bottom line of the horn first, going from right to left. Then, add a curl above the ear; this point angles in front of the others, so it must be drawn first. Afterward, draw the other antler points behind it and connect the line back to the top of the head. Repeat the process for the right antler, then erase your sketch lines.

HIGH-FLYING
CRYPTIDS

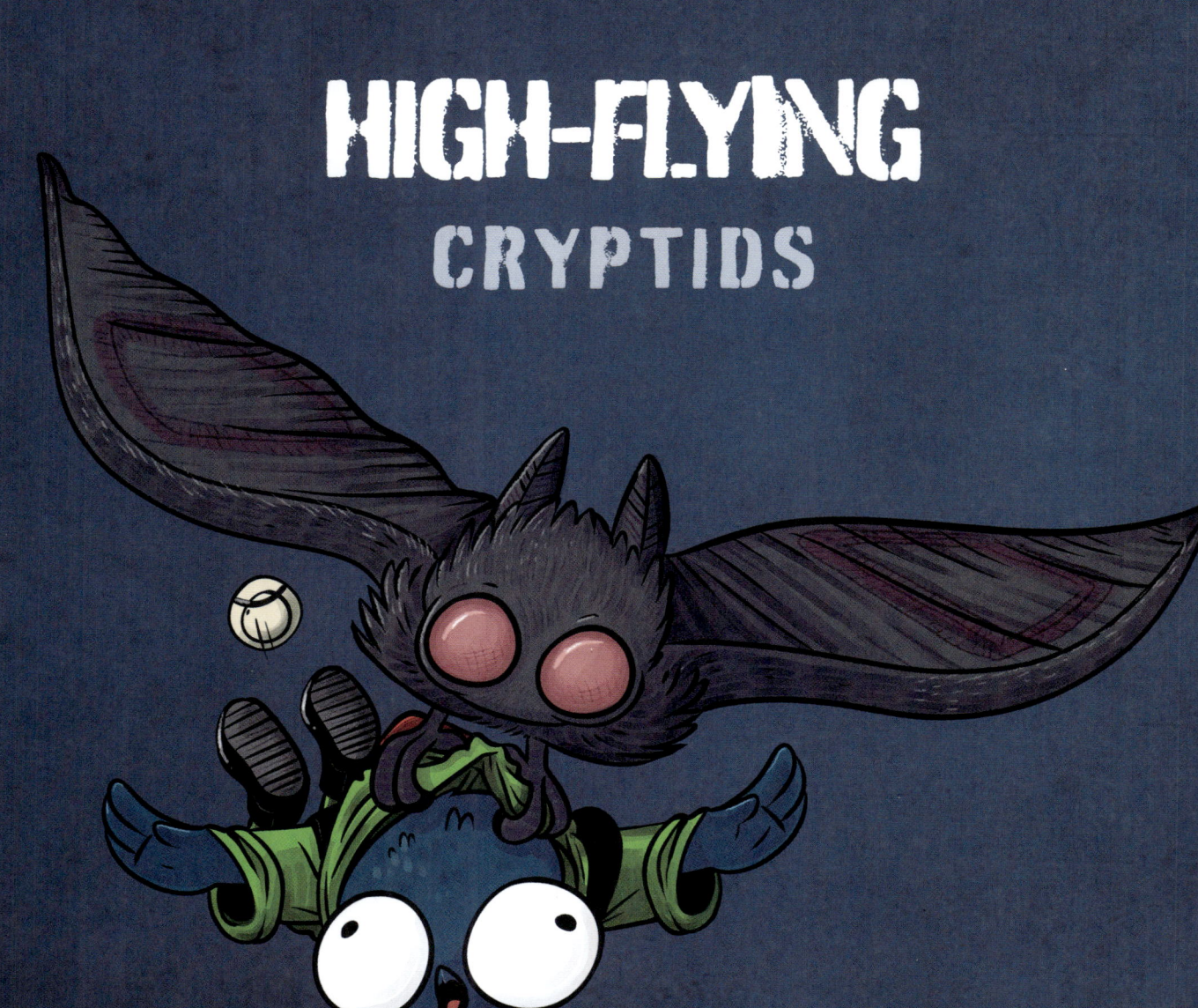

Spotted shooting across the sky, flying cryptids remain high in the air and out of sight. Most who witness these cryptids recount a large shadow passing over them or a strange blur in the sky. Living in trees, atop mountains, inside abandoned structures, or even in outer space, the cryptids in this chapter have one thing in common: the ability to fly. With feathery wings, leathery membranes, or high-tech equipment, many strange organisms have been seen flying and falling from the sky.

Mothman

The first sighting of Mothman occurred on November 15, 1966, in Point Pleasant, West Virginia, United States. Four witnesses were driving past an abandoned WWII munitions plant when they passed what looked like a man. Shadowy, thin, yet muscular, the seven-foot-tall (2 m) figure unfurled a pair of large wings. It turned and stared at the witnesses with its glowing red, hypnotic eyes. Frightened, they sped away. The monster flew above their car, effortlessly keeping up with them. It screeched as it followed them to the city limits.

Over the next several days, numerous residents caught a glimpse of the creature. After a year of sightings later, the Silver Bridge in the town of Point Pleasant collapsed, resulting in the death of forty-six people. Mothman was not seen again after the event. This led to some believing that the sightings of the creature and the collapse of the bridge were linked.

Sketch an oval. To the left of the oval's
center, add a curved, vertical guideline.
Then, sketch a curved, horizontal guideline
near the bottom of the shape.

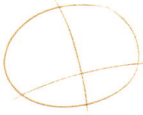

Using your guidelines, draw two round
eyes with a curve on the side. Above each
eye, draw a small, angry eyebrow. Lastly,
draw an angle below your horizontal
guideline to create a mouth.

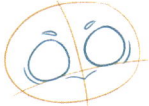

Draw a wavy, pointed antenna on top of each
side of the circle; they should look like they
are quivering in the breeze. In the center,
draw a line down the middle that curves with
the shape of each antenna. Then, add a few
angled dashes on each side of the antennae
that point down toward the center.

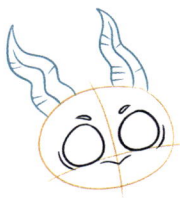

TIP

This Mothman has a simple bull's-eye in
the middle of its wings. Customize your
Mothman's wings by creating a pattern
or referencing a real moth's design.

4

Connect the antennae with a V. On
each side of the head, follow the curve
of your sketch and draw a line that
swoops away and squiggles, forming
a few rounded points of fur. Continue
to add curving lines of fur below. Then,
erase your sketch lines and create two
lines to start the legs.

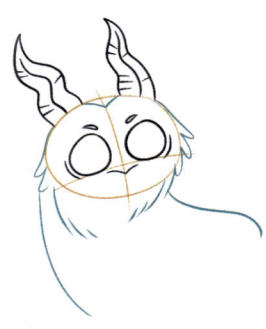

5

Draw the outer part of the lower leg
on each side. Draw the inner legs by
mirroring the outer legs. Between the
two limbs, add a swooping curve under
the neck that joins the two together.
Then, at the top of each side of the
head, draw a swooping arch that rounds
up and down into a squarish shape.

6

Inside the square shape at the top
of the left wing, draw a long, curving
line that reaches under the left leg.
From left to right, connect both sides
of the wing with curves of varying
size; each curve should form one
thick, round feather.

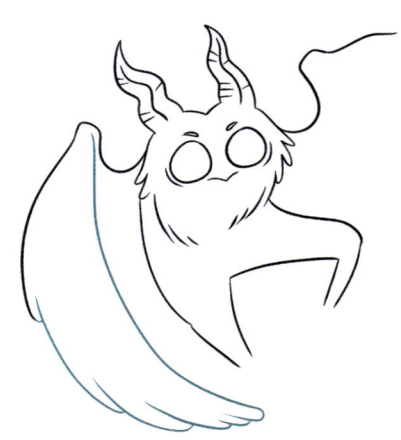

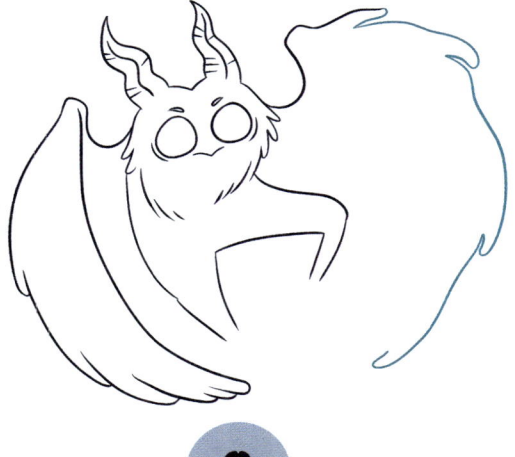

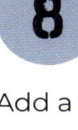

7

While the left wing is curled, the right wing is spread open. Draw a continuous, wavering line at the end of your right wing's line. Make the wing a curving, semioval shape overall, and periodically add large, round feathers in your line.

8

Add a foot below each leg. The Mothman has three-toed claws like a bird. Beside the left foot, draw an angle to show that the wing passes behind the foot. Below and between the feet, finish the right wing. Draw four long, wide, and round feathers; the leftmost feather should curl up and behind the left foot.

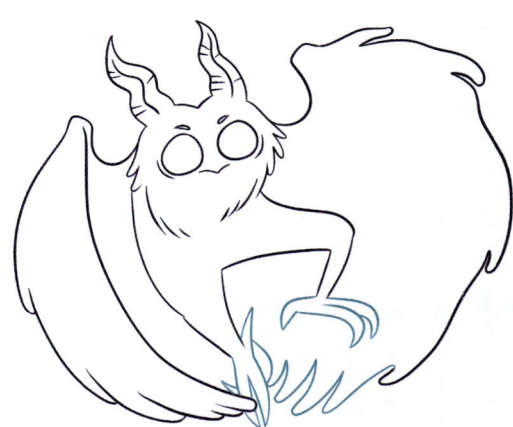

9

Draw dashes and short, curved lines on the creature's body to give it a hairy texture. Add more lines around the knees and neck. Afterward, draw a curve at the end of each toe to make claws. Next, add a pattern in the center of each wing; draw a wavy circle with smaller rings inside. Scatter round curves, U shapes, and differently sized Ws on both wings.

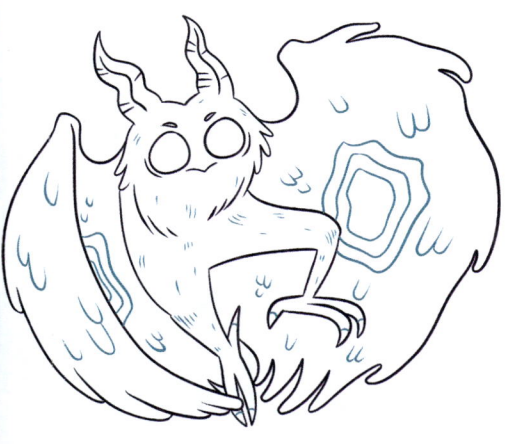

Flatwoods Monster

On September 12, 1952, the inhabitants of a small town called Flatwoods in West Virginia, United States, watched the sky as something bright red fell and landed atop a hill on a nearby farm. A group of onlookers decided to go see what it was. The party smelled something before they saw anything. A faint, pungent mist obscured the ground and made them feel sick. Farther up the hill, they saw a fiery red light beaming down from above. Before them was a tall, twenty-five-foot-long (8 m), metallic object. Next to the object was a ten-foot-tall (3 m) creature.

Looking down at them, the creature was six feet (2 m) tall and clothed in rubberized silk that hung in drapes. The alien jolted toward the witnesses and spewed mist. When others arrived to investigate, nothing remained on top of the hill but matted grass, burn marks, a thick, black substance, and a nauseating smell.

Sketch a teardrop shape. Near the bottom, draw a circle inside. Within the circle, sketch a vertical guideline through its center and a horizontal guideline below the center.

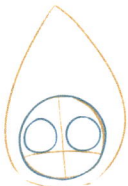

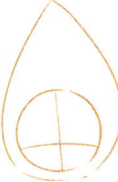

Trace your circle sketch from Step 1, then draw two round eyes on each side of your vertical guideline. The eyes should be near the side of the head; their bottoms should rest on the horizontal guideline.

Draw an outward-facing angle on the bottom left and right sides of the head. Using your sketch as a guide, draw a shape like a spade around the head that attaches to each new line. The spade should have a tall, sharp point and be round at the bottom.

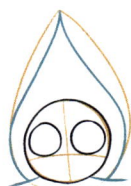

TIP

The city of Flatwoods has commissioned and displayed several Flatwoods Monster chairs that are shaped and painted like the creature. The huge wooden seats have become an American tourist attraction.

4

Erase your sketch lines. Then, draw a line from one side of the shoulders to the other, making a squarish, blocky shape with rounded corners. Draw a large V shape under the head. Then, draw a U shape above it.

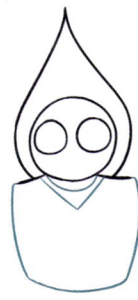

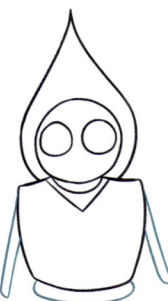

5

Under the torso, draw a round belt that bubbles outward. Next, draw a long, angled, sticklike arm on each side of the body. The limbs should start at the edge of each shoulder and reach down to the belt.

6

Under each arm, add a round, triangular joint. Draw another long, rectangular shape on the left, but angle it away from the body. Repeat the shape on the right, pointing it in the opposite direction.

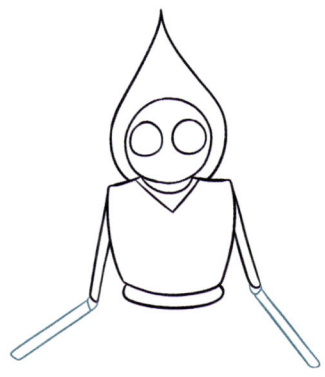

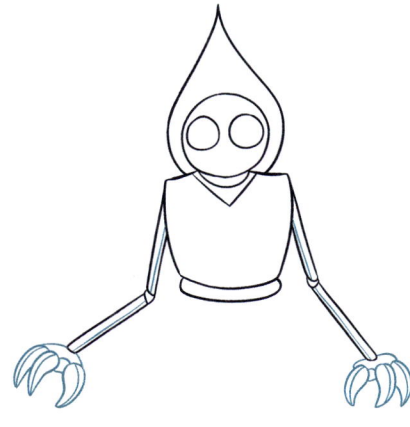

Draw a line that matches the angle of each arm piece on the inner edge of each limb. After, add a three-clawed hand to each arm. The claws are an upside-down teardrop shape and curve in opposite directions.

Above the eyes, draw an angry unibrow shaped like a V. Below, extend the bottom of each eye and add a horizontal line to create a blocky nose. Under the nose, draw a frown; on each side, add an angle pointed toward the nose. Draw the lip and round chin.

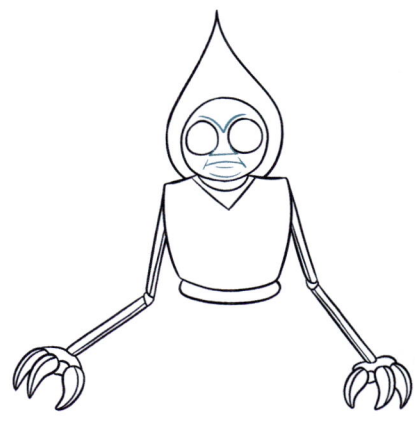

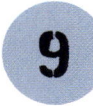

Draw a triangle in the center of the belt. On each side of the belt, draw two long lines that curve at the top and swoop outward at the bottom to create a dress-like shape. Connect the two sides of the alien's garment at the bottom with a wavy line. Next, draw curvy lines under the belt that match the dress's flow. Add lines of various lengths.

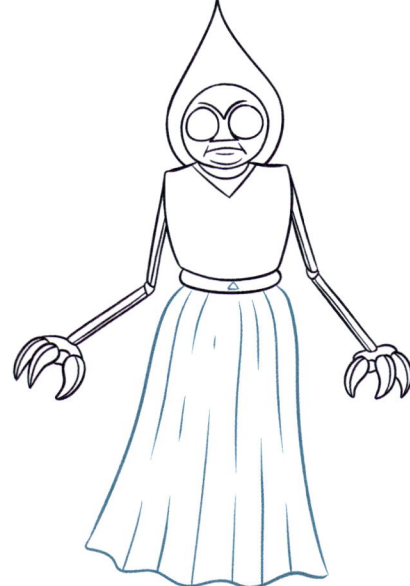

Thunderbird

Traditionally, the Thunderbird is a birdlike spirit in Indigenous mythology that is often associated with storms and lightning. A subject in several cultures' stories, the Thunderbird varies from group to group in physique and personality. In some stories, the creature creates lightning by blinking and thunder by flapping its wings; in other tales, it fights evil beasts, controls the weather, or delivers messages. Witness accounts are scattered throughout the American Southwest, the Great Lakes area, eastern Canada, and northeastern America.

Whereas the Indigenous Thunderbird is an occasionally benevolent entity, the Thunderbird means something entirely different to non-Indigenous Peoples. To them, the Thunderbird is an unidentified bird of extraordinary size. Since the nineteenth century, witnesses across North America have claimed to see a giant, black, eagle-like bird. Lacking a moniker, the cryptid bird was misappropriately dubbed the Thunderbird. Other sightings claim the creature has a reptilian face, a featherless head, and a white ring around its neck.

Sketch a teardrop shape that points to the left.

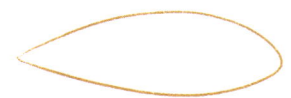

Draw the bird's neck, head, and beak on the right side of your shape. This line is curvy with three hills, each lower than the last. At its end, turn the curve into a vertical line that lies above the bottom of your shape. Below, draw the beak's tip and wavering frown that nearly meets with your sketch. Under it, draw a gentle slope to the left.

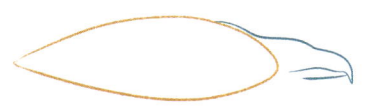

On the second hill of the head, draw a curvy line to the left that attaches to the mouth's frown. Draw a nostril to the right. To the left of the beak, draw the Thunderbird's eyebrow and eye. Extend the bottom of the beak to the neck by drawing a gently sloping line that transitions into a few round, curving feathers.

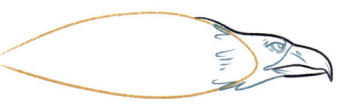

TIP

Thunderbirds are associated with severe thunderstorms. Try drawing large, fluffy storm clouds, rain, or lightning around your Thunderbird.

4

Use your sketch as a guide to draw the creature's chest and leg. The leg angles out from the belly, ending in a tuft of overlapping feathers. The leftmost feather curves up, whereas the others curl down.

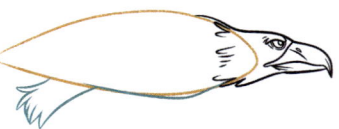

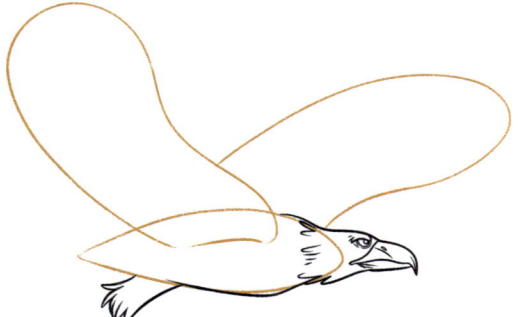

5

Sketch the wings, which are bean-like, round shapes.

6

Draw the left wing. Begin on the lower right and trace your sketch. Diverge from your sketch near the top of the wing and draw a series of long, oblong feathers. On the upper left side of the wing, follow your sketch and draw a wobbly line. Then draw the right wing.

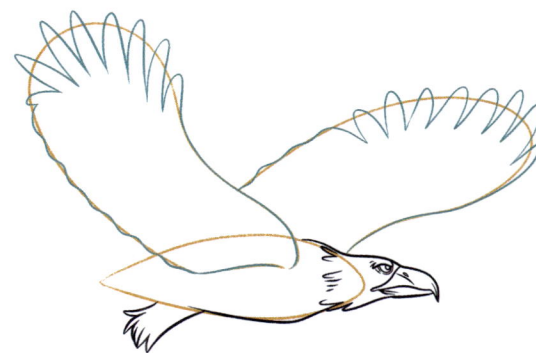

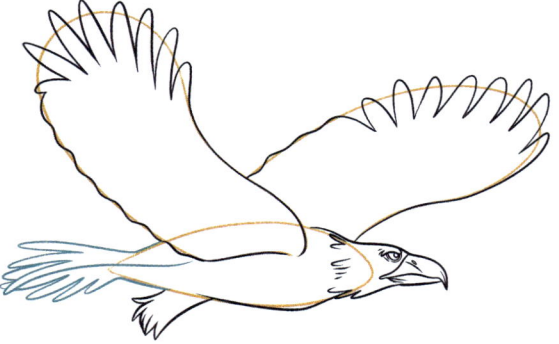

7

Draw the Thunderbird's tail feathers with a series of long, curving lines. Extend the center line onto the body.

8

Erase your sketch lines, then draw the feet. Under Step 4's leg, add the first foot. Starting with the thumb, draw its long, curling claw, then add the lower two toes. These two toes overlap, and their claws pass behind the thumb. Above the thumb, draw a short, round curve to the right. Next, add a left-pointing feather to create the other leg. To the right of the foot, draw the curve of this obscured foot's toes.

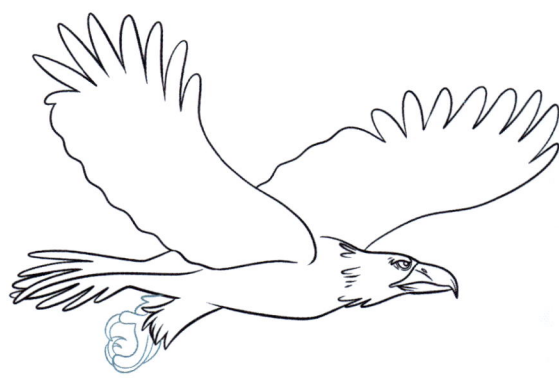

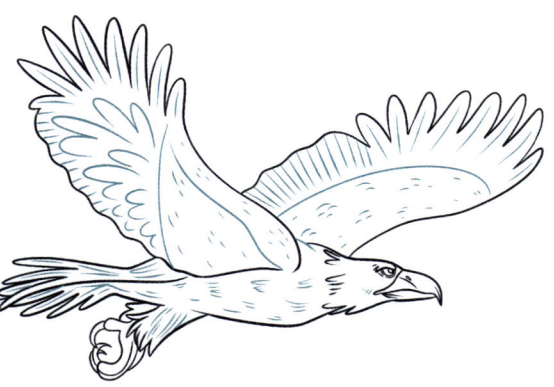

9

Use a series of curves and straight lines to give the impression that the feathers on the Thunderbird have different textures depending on the part of its body: the wings, beak, legs, and tail.

Wolpertinger

The Wolpertinger is a chimera from the alpine forests of Germany. Parts rabbit, squirrel, deer, and pheasant, it is a strange sight to behold. Most stories describe the animal as a rabbit or squirrel with large horns, tall ears, a deer's tail, large, fluffy wings, and sometimes two big, sharp fangs that poke from the upper lip. Some believe that an illness called cottontail rabbit papillomavirus may have inspired the creation of the cryptid. The virus causes hornlike growths near the mouth or on top of the head, transforming the rabbit into a seemingly horned or vampiric beast.

The Wolpertinger is a hoax animal like the jackalope, and many artisans, folklore enthusiasts, and con artists have tried their hand at Wolpertinger taxidermy. A few examples are currently displayed in museum exhibits, such as at the German Hunting and Fishing Museum in Munich.

1

Sketch a circle. Under it, sketch a rectangle.

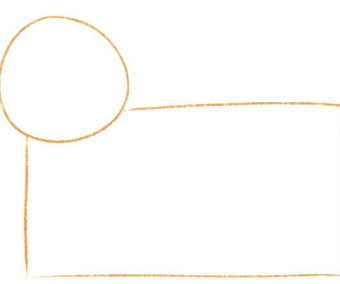

2

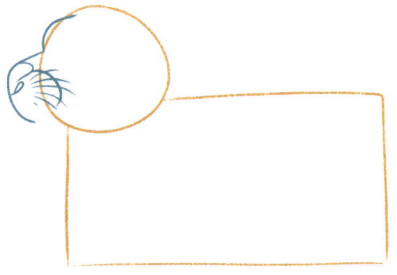

On the top left of your circle, draw the forehead and snout; while the forehead barely curves past the sketch, the snout extends far past it. At the top left of the snout, add a nose, nostril, cheek, and whiskers.

3

On top of the head, draw a smaller curve that matches the forehead. From each bump, draw a long and short eyebrow hair that curves upward. To the right of the snout, draw a curve to the left. Under the snout, draw the mouth and chin. Draw the Wolpertinger's fangs, then its lower jaw and neck. On the lower right side of your circle, draw the back of the rabbit's head.

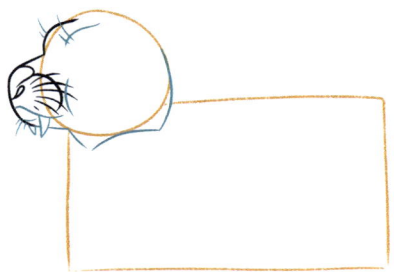

TIP

Once you've completed the Wolpertinger, try creating your own chimera! Swap out some of this cryptid's body parts with another animal's as you redo the tutorial.

4

Draw a tall rabbit ear on the top right side of the head. The ear is squarish at the bottom, round in the middle, and comes to a round point at the top. Next, draw the overlapping inner ear.

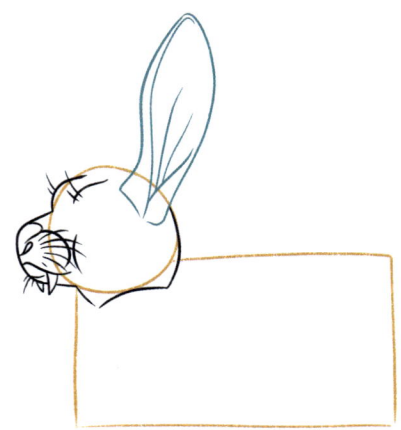

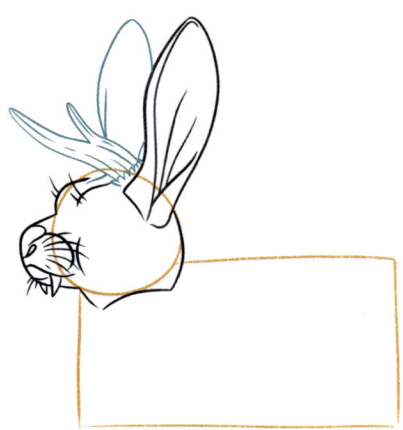

5

Add an antler. Under the antler, draw a short, curvy line. Above the antler, draw the other ear and add a vertical stretch line to its left side.

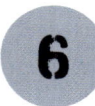

6

Behind Step 5's antler, draw the second antler; copy its shape and texture, making it smaller. Next, draw and color in a circle that is under the eyebrow and above the cheek. Add a short, diagonal dash on the side of the eye. Above and below the eye, draw a small curve.

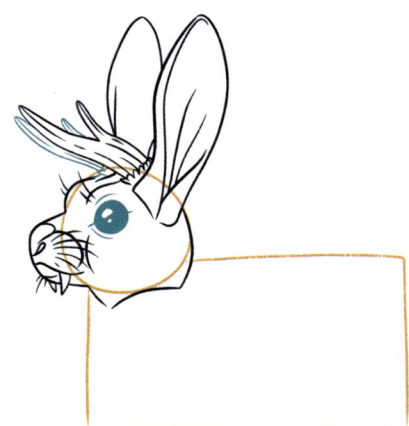

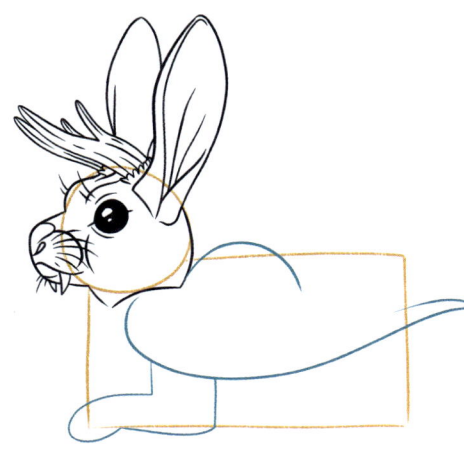

Below the creature's head, draw its wing with curvy and swooping lines. Under the left side of the wing, draw an arm. Held at a right angle, the forearm curves into a round paw.

Under the head, draw squiggly lines of fur. Draw the Wolpertinger's two front paws. At the bottom of your rectangle sketch, draw a line from the elbow to the end of the box. Then, on the end of the Wolpertinger's wing, draw a series of round, overlapping curves to create feathers. Add the Wolpertinger's back foot.

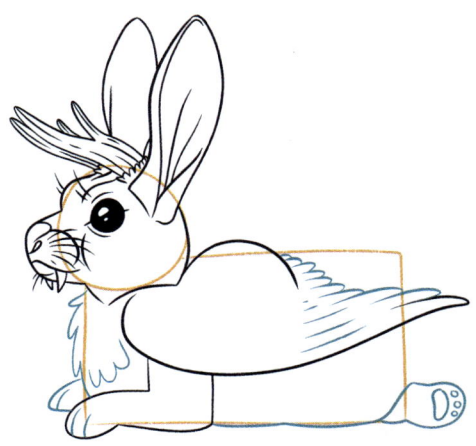

Erase your sketch lines. Above the foot, draw the tail. Inside, draw several lines that match its curve; include a variety of line lengths. Next, between the head and upper left side of the wing, draw a small curve. Then, copy the front wing's squiggly, feathery lines above it in two rows.

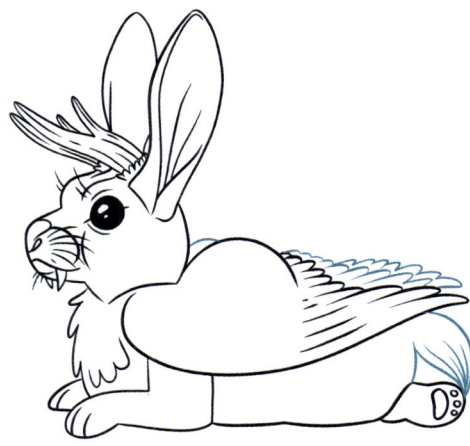

Snallygaster

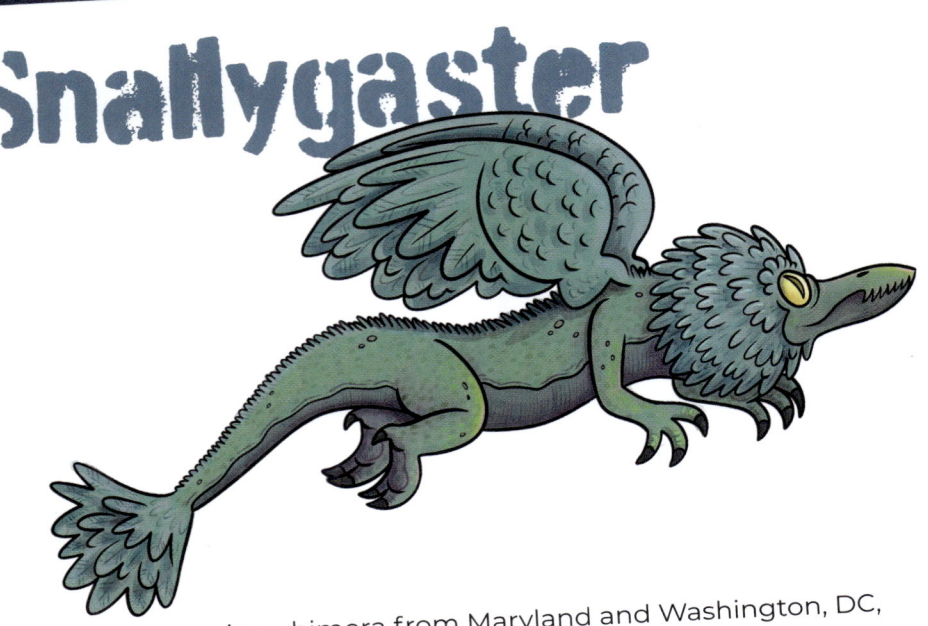

The Snallygaster is a chimera from Maryland and Washington, DC, United States. Part bird, part reptile, it possesses hooked claws, a serpentine body, and a large eyeball in the middle of its forehead. The cryptid takes many forms, sometimes having feathery or leathery wings. Its mouth has been described as an elongated bird's bill, like the maw of a dragon, or like metallic pinchers. Sometimes the chimera is given a wreath of tentacles around its head; other times it is depicted with a feathery crest. Nevertheless, most accounts state that it has a scaly body, insatiable hunger, and a call like a train whistle.

Sightings began in the eighteenth century. While the monster was dangerous, folklore states the demonic beast could be warded away with seven-pointed stars. The symbols can still be viewed on barns in Maryland.

1

Sketch a circle. To the right and in the middle, sketch a pointy triangle. Draw a wavy line at the top of your circle, extending to the left.

2

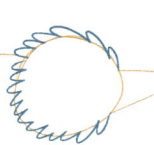

Using your circle as a guide, draw a squiggly line around the shape.

3

Where your triangle and circle meet, draw an oval. Inside, draw a sharp pupil. Above the eye, draw a feathery eyebrow. To the right of the eye, draw a curve.

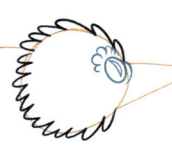

TIP

The Snallygaster was first described as a horrific, blood-drinking monster; it was originally named Schneller Geist, or "quick ghost" in German.

4

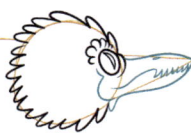

Draw the beak. Starting at the top of the eyelid, draw a curving line that ends at the point of your triangle sketch. From there, draw another curving line below that ends with a round feather. To the right, add a semicircle and a small curve that follows the eye. Then, draw a zigzagging line near the beak's tip to make teeth. The last fang should curl up and back to create a smile. The curve should end before reaching the left side of the beak. Lastly, draw a nostril on the beak.

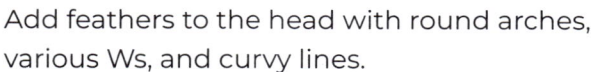

5

Add feathers to the head with round arches, various Ws, and curvy lines.

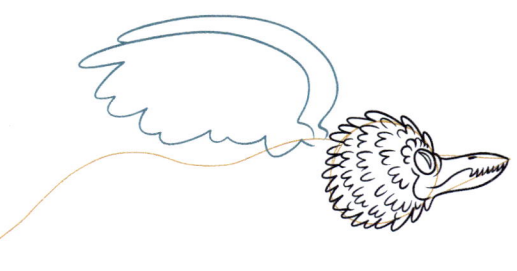

6

Behind the head, draw a pair of wings. Beginning with the leftmost wing, draw a bump on top of your sketched line. From it, draw a larger, wider curve to the left. Below, add a curvy line made of round shapes and bumps to the right, ending below where you started, but not connecting. Copy the top of this wing to the right.

7

Along your sketched line, draw tiny squiggles to make small, thin, upright feathers along the Snallygaster's back.

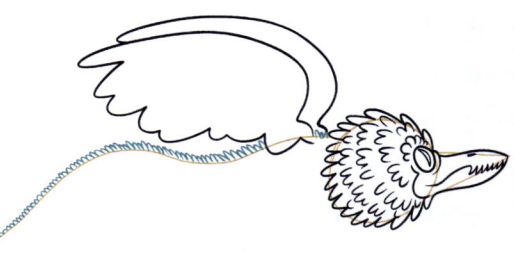

8

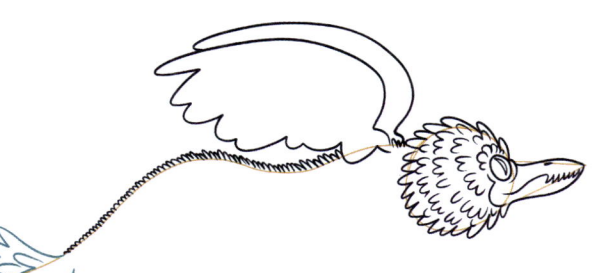

At the end of your sketched line, draw a tail that fans out with feathers. Draw two rows of feathers inside with curves, round arches, and Ws.

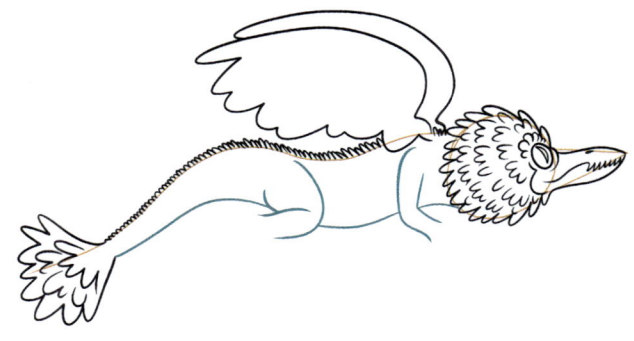

9

Below the left wing, draw an arm. The limb has a round shoulder and reaches below the creature's head, angling to the right. The arm's elbow is rounded, and its inner lines are sharp. Then, to the left of the wing's center, draw the back leg. Begin with a backward C under the wing; to the new line's left, add a small curve near its center and a horizontal curve below. Afterward, connect the tail to the back leg with a curvy line; match the twist and curve of the back. Do the same between the arm and leg, and the arm and head.

10

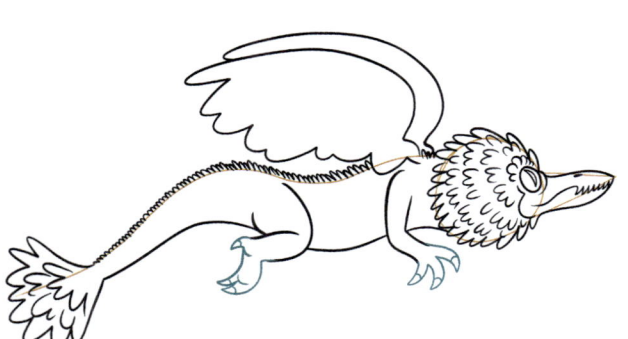

Next, draw a three-clawed hand and foot, one at the front and one at the back of the Snallygaster. The hand is stretched under the head; add a curve near the end of each finger to make claws. Each finger is the same size.

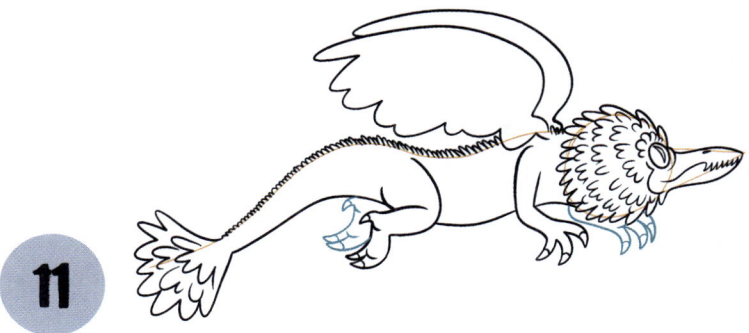

11

Add an arm and leg to the other side of the cryptid. Repeat Step 10 and copy the foot to the left and the hand to the right. While the second foot is identical to the first, the right hand's claws are closer together, are partially obscured, and the hand has a curve on its palm.

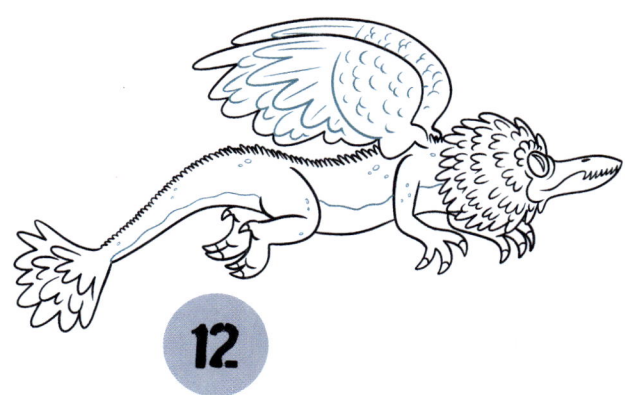

12

Erase your sketch lines and add texture, such as along the cryptid's body. Use rounded lines and Ws to add feathers to the Snallygaster's wings.

ACKNOWLEDGMENTS

This book is dedicated to my family, who have always encouraged and believed in my passions and eccentric interests.

To my partner, for being my greatest, most patient supporter and willing to help in any way, no matter how strange.

To the cryptid community, for their love, inspiration, and unbelievable support.

To my BCWPA Agents, who make my art worth making.

Lastly, thank you to my editor, Elizabeth, and the Quarto Group, who gave me the opportunity to create this fun book—and transformed my jumble of pictures and words into something cohesive.

ABOUT THE AUTHOR

Ballyraven is an Appalachian illustrator who loves nature and monsters. A traditional artist, she predominantly works with pencils, dip pens, and inks to create wildlife field sketches, medieval bestiary pages, and other art for books, games, and cryptid enthusiasts. Through her work, she shares her love for prehistory, science, fantasy, and all things creepy. Ballyraven not only draws but also writes books and hosts a podcast—all focused on cryptids, myths, and the paranormal.

FIND BALLYRAVEN ONLINE
For process photos and more art, follow:
www.instagram.com/ballyraven_folklore

For more information on cryptids, myths, and folklore, visit:
www.ballyraven.com

For questions, tutorials, and a cryptid community, join Ballyraven on Patreon:
www.patreon.com/ballyraven